Praise for C

'The most enchanting cat book ever'

Jilly Cooper

'A chaotic, hilarious and heart-wrenching love affair with this most characterful of feline breeds'

The People's Friend

'If you read *Cats in the Belfry* the first time round, be prepared to be enchanted all over again. If you haven't, then expect to laugh out loud, shed a few tears and be totally captivated by Doreen's stories of her playful and often naughty Siamese cats'

Your Cat **magazine**

'An invasion of mice prompted Tovey and her husband to acquire a cat – or rather for Sugieh to acquire them. A beautiful Siamese, Sugieh turned out to be a tempestuous, iron-willed prima donna who soon had her running circles around her. And that's before she had kittens! A funny and poignant reflection of life with a Siamese, that is full of cheer'

The Good Book Guide

'*Cats in the Belfry* will ring bells with anyone who's ever been charmed – or driven to distraction – by a feline'

The Weekly News

'A warm, witty and moving cat classic. A must for all cat lovers'

Living for Retirement

Praise for *Cats in May*

'If you loved Doreen Tovey's *Cats in the Belfry* you won't want to miss the sequel, *Cats in May*.

The Toveys attempt to settle down to a quiet life in the country but, unfortunately for them, their tyrannical Siamese cats have other ideas. From causing an uproar on the BBC to staying out all night, Sheba and Solomon's outrageous behaviour leaves the Toveys at their wits' end. This witty and stylish tale will have animal lovers giggling to the very last page'

Your Cat magazine

'No-one writes about cats with more wit, humour and affection than Doreen Tovey. Every word is a delight!'

The People's Friend

Praise for *The New Boy*

'Delightful stories of Tovey's irrepressible Siamese cats'

Publishing News

DOUBLE TROUBLE

DOREEN TOVEY

summersdale

DOUBLE TROUBLE

Michael Joseph edition published 1972.
Bantam edition published 1994.

This edition published by Summersdale Publishers Ltd in 2007.

Summersdale Publishers Ltd
46 West Street
Chichester
West Sussex
PO19 1RP
UK

www.summersdale.com

Printed and bound in Great Britain.

ISBN: 1-84024-569-7
ISBN 13: 978-1-84024-569-1

Also by Doreen Tovey

Cats in the Belfry
Cats in May
The New Boy
Donkey Work
Life with Grandma
Raining Cats and Donkeys
Making the Horse Laugh
The Coming of Saska
A Comfort of Cats
Roses Round the Door
Waiting in the Wings
More Cats in the Belfry
Cats in Concord

One

TIME PASSES, EVEN IN a quiet country backwater such as ours. Sheba, our blue-point Siamese, was now a staid old lady of sixteen. Solomon Secundus, better known as Seeley, whom we'd bought to comfort her and us after our first great Solomon died, was a strapping young Seal Point of eighteen months. Annabel, our donkey, was nine...

Not that she looked it, mind you. Not that she acted like it, either. As I start this book it is with a thumb that feels as though it will never be the same again, thanks to Annabel's idea of a joke.

It so happened that one Monday morning Charles decided to put her out to graze in the Forestry lane which adjoins the cottage – Monday being when the local riding school takes its day off, so there was no chance of her pursuing her favourite pastime of holding the horses at bay by stretching her tether rope across in front of them.

It also happened that there were, that morning, two private individuals out riding. The first one, whom we didn't know, Annabel let go by without hindrance. When I looked over the gate to check on her she was eating innocently from the side to which she was tethered, neck stretched industriously up to reach a bramble, small rounded bottom tucked neatly out of the way, without so much as a glance at the passing horse.

When the second rider came by, however – and this one was known to us all right; a certain young lady who rode round the place with the air of Elizabeth the First making one of her progresses and she hoped we yokels appreciated it... when she came on the scene Annabel was eating, apparently quite by accident, from the opposite hedge, with her rope stretched tight across the lane like a customs barrier.

'She *would*,' I said when Charles, who'd come tearing down from the orchard, said Annabel was holding up the Robart girl and would I come and help him shift her. Which was why, mortified at the thought of the spectacle we were going to present trying to move that little so-and-so while the other one sat her horse and watched us, I rushed out, not stopping to pick up Annabel's bridle (without which, small as she is, one might as well try to move Mahomet's mountain), untied her tether rope and tried to pull her out of the way on that.

The spectacle began without delay. Annabel reared like a Lippitzer, I fell down in the mud, my shoe came off and, as I got up, Annabel came waltzing backwards and trod on my poor bare foot.

'You all right?' enquired Charles, who would ask that, I have no doubt, if I were falling straight down the crater of Vesuvius.

I didn't trust myself to reply.

'Grab her collar!' I muttered between anguished teeth. 'Grab her *collar*, or she'll start playing up again.'

Thrusting my foot into a mud-filled shoe, doing my best not to limp and grasping Annabel in a grip of iron by one side of her collar while Charles held her firmly by the other, we led her towards her field. There was a patch near her gate where the lane was even muddier and it was necessary to skirt it in single file along the hillside; I in front, Annabel in the middle and Charles, trying to look insouciant, in the rear. And there, finding it difficult to keep his balance while holding her from behind, Charles let go of her collar, Annabel kicked up her heels and shot back down to the lane and I, the victim as usual of the pair of them, was hauled down behind her like a donkey cart.

I let go of her collar too, of course. But her tether rope was round my thumb, I couldn't get it loose, and although I ran like mad the moment came when Annabel was running faster than I was; only the fact that I eventually tripped, sat down in the road and so acted as a drag anchor on our dear little donkey prevented my being towed up the hill like a kite.

'You all right?' enquired Charles, passing me at the double to retrieve the cause of it all.

I left him to put Annabel into her field. I left him to accept the casual 'Thank you' of the imperturbable Miss Robart. (Imperturbable or not, Charles said even she looked slightly stunned as she went past.) I, with as much dignity as I could muster, hobbled into the cottage to nurse my anguished thumb, which felt about two feet long, and ponder why on earth we kept a donkey when we had two Siamese cats.

It is a matter of circumstances, of course. There are times when I wonder why we keep Siamese cats. But at the moment Seeley – safely in custody for once instead of playing hookey in the woods with our wondering where on earth to look for him first – was sitting on a table closing his eyes at me with such an air of concern as to indicate that he was my only friend in the world and by gosh, he knew how it hurt.

He did at that. Only a few weeks previously Annabel had gummed up his thumbs, too. On that occasion, galloping round the lawn to show off to some passers-by, she'd put one of her feet down the clock-golf hole, trod on the metal lining and, by dint of the fact that she weighed, galloping, about half a ton, had turned down the edge of it like a razor. This we'd deduced following the horrifying discovery one morning that Seeley now had completely flat thumb pads. We'd practically had the Crime Squad on the job till we remembered his addiction to lying on his stomach fishing the ball out of the clock-golf hole with his paws – and sure enough there, when Charles went out to look, was a set of familiar gallop-prints going right across the hole and a sharp metal edge inside.

My, that must have hurt, I said, examining the poor little sawn-off pads. They were healing now. It must have been a couple of days since he'd done it. But they were still pretty red and sore-looking. Like Solomon, who'd once been distinguishable as the only cat in the district with a forked tongue as a result of howling at his opponent in a cat-fight and inadvertently biting through it, Seeley would now be distinguishable as the only cat around with flat-topped thumbs.

He'd squeezed his eyes at me on that occasion, too. Hardly even noticed it, he said.

All Siamese have their idiosyncrasies and though Seeley was so much like Solomon that many of their habits were identical, this business of meaningful eye-closing was entirely Seeley's own. It conveyed wisdom, innocence, apology, affection – whichever he meant it to do at the moment. Tight-squeezed eyes when I was nursing my thumb meant sympathy. Tight-squeezed eyes when I was demanding Who'd made all those footmarks on the refrigerator meant he just couldn't think, it must have been Sheba – though Sheba was far too frail these days to do any climbing and there was only one cat around who made footprints two inches across. Tight-squeezed eyes when a visitor spoke to him meant he was very pleased to meet them – and ensured, seeing that it produced a more Oriental expression than ever, that they remarked how striking he was. He was indeed. His mask was the darkest seal imaginable, his eyes the most vivid, slanting blue. He was huge and broad-shouldered – a king among cats. Only – which sometimes produced a more striking effect than ever – *he* still thought he was a kitten.

He still couldn't open the hall door, for instance. He expected Sheba to open it for him. And while in his young days it had been an endearing sight to see her pushing practisedly through with a fat little kitten hard on her heels, it looked odd, to say the least, to see her still frailly doing it at sixteen while a positive young Hercules of a cat waited to jump over her head as soon as she'd made a gap.

He still used his baby voice, too. True he could roar like a buffalo when he wanted to – when we wouldn't let him out, for instance, or there was fish for supper and he was wailing about how he loathed it. But normally he went round conversing in little 'Woohs' and 'Mrrr-mrrs', and he didn't fight, and he never ever sprayed... He'd been neutered at six months old, of course, and wouldn't have sprayed in the house – but, outdoors, our first Solomon had been quite outstanding for his spraying. He'd sprayed to mark his territory. He'd sprayed just to show that he could. 'Proper liddle water-pistol' our neighbour Father Adams had once said admiringly. That was when he was spraying Miss Wellington's gatepost, of course, not Father Adams's own.

Seeley did none of these things. We put it down to his being with Sheba. She was so old, we thought, it probably made Seeley feel like a kitten beside her. Being Sheba she no doubt treated him as one, too. Told him to sit down; be Quiet, she wanted to rest; it was a fact that she could quell him with a glance.

Sometimes we felt that he was missing out on his youth... at his age Sheba and Solomon had whizzed round the place like fireflies. But we couldn't get him a young companion while our faithful old girl was with us. Siamese have very strange temperaments. Pushed into the background she might have felt unwanted and decided to die.

So, that last winter, we continued. Making a fuss of her. Letting her out whenever she asked, which made her feel very important indeed. Old or not, she still liked putting one over on Seeley and very much the senior prefect she was when, after a late-night stroll up the garden with Charles and a look with him through the gate, she came in to sit by the fire, purring, fresh-furred, with a look at the envious Seeley which informed him that *he* was still a child. Only she was allowed out after dark.

She had priority at milk-time too. At ten o'clock sharp every night she climbed on my lap, tapped me on the cheek with a soft but urgent paw and, when she'd got my attention, fixed me with a look that meant Milk. In the kitchen. Now. She made no sound when reminding me. That, as she and I both knew, would have had Seeley clamouring for His Too in an instant. Silently I proceeded to the kitchen. Silently Sheba accompanied me. She sat on the kitchen stool, drank two saucerfuls of cream off the top of the bottle – and only then was Seeley, by this time bawling his head off because we were Missing and He Knew what we were Doing, allowed tearfully out to join her in a third.

Thus we made her feel that she was wanted. And Seeley, when there wasn't a question of food involved, made her feel wanted too. He would assiduously seek her out when he came in from his outings... Mrr-mrr-mrring about where was she and he hadn't seen her for ages – while Sheba, if it was one of her better days, would Mrr-mrr encouragingly at him back. He would wash her when he was feeling benevolent – not much of a wash it was true, since Seeley, like Solomon before him, didn't go much for the cleaning lark. A lick or two behind her ears, a slurp on the top of the head that nearly laid her flat on the

15

floor... 'Not bad, is she?' he'd demand, sitting proudly by her side like a pavement artist while Sheba, pleased with such attention, would close her eyes and purr.

He slept with her at night; he spent hours during the day sitting with her in front of the fire or on the settee – because he loved her but also, it must be admitted, because he liked sharing the hotwater bottle she now had continuously in her bed. And thereby hangs another tale, because hitherto we'd always used aluminium bottles, which couldn't be smashed like stone ones, or punctured by claws as could rubber.

They can still be damaged by constant dropping, however. Over the years, our nerves shattered by cats climbing our backs while we were filling them or staging what sounded like the French Revolution suddenly starting up upstairs, we'd demolished bottle after bottle. And one night, harassed by Seeley shouting for his supper in one ear and the pressure cooker with his rabbit in it suddenly letting off steam in the other, I dropped the last metal bottle just once too often and that was that. When I tried to replace it I was told they weren't making them any longer; most people have electric blankets.

Most people maybe, but not cats with Siamese claws. We didn't want them electrocuting themselves in the night. For days I hunted in case somewhere there was a shop with an old-fashioned metal bottle under its counter, but it was no use. So eventually I bought a rubber one.

Sheba wouldn't stick her claws in it, I assured the doubtful Charles. She was too old now for that. And if we put a double layer of rug on top of it Seeley wasn't really likely to puncture it either. If he did, in any case, they'd jump off straight away. No cats in their right minds would sit on a leaking bottle.

Saying which I filled it, put it down before the fire inside the bed on which they slept at night – and Seeley, advancing cautiously towards it, said he wasn't going to sit on it at all.

It smelled, he said, putting his nose to the rug with exaggerated, long-necked suspicion. It Wobbled, he announced, standing on it with his two front paws and quivering violently to prove his point. It was Dangerous, he finally decided and, being Seeley and knowing no fear, he raked the rug away so that he could see the bottle better. Presumably in case it attacked.

It was like having an obsessional bomb disposer around the place. As fast as I covered the bottle with the rug, Seeley, his whiskers bushed for action, intently exposed it again. Eventually, thinking he'd give up if we left him in darkness, Charles and I went to bed. Covering the bottle once more, of course, and adjuring him to be good.

We should have known better. Seeley, when he gets an idea in his head, sticks to it like a leech. During the night he dismantled it all over again. This time, so that nobody could possibly sit on it by mistake, he pulled away the rug and the various sweaters which made up their bed, strewed them widely in all directions and left the bottle lying bleakly in the middle of the hearthrug.

There we found it in the morning. There we found Sheba, too, huddled forlornly in the fireplace complaining that she hadn't slept a wink all night. Seeley, still on guard, sat watchfully on the table. It was entirely thanks to him it hadn't gone off, he said.

Two

IT WAS QUITE A while before he trusted that hot water bottle. For several nights, so that Sheba could sleep on it undisturbed, we had taken him to bed with us. Stretched full length under the bedclothes, his head on the pillow, his eyes squeezed tight in utter bliss – I can't pretend that he worried then about his girlfriend's safety. Could this but last for Ever was obviously Seeley's solitary thought.

Eventually he did get used to the bottle, however, and there he was once more, curled up on it at night, sitting on it by Sheba's side, importantly, during the day. He was tremendously fond of our old girl, as I realised particularly after the incident of his cage. This was the temporary affair we'd put on the lawn the previous summer, after he'd been bitten by an adder. He'd spent many a morning in there with Sheba, safeguarded from jumping on things that wriggled while we got on with our work.

It had, in fact, become an accepted part of his routine. A trek up the Forestry lane before the sun was up, a sniff round Annabel's paddock to make sure there was nothing interesting there, a sortie into the woods, perhaps, for a peer down one or two holes... and then, when I called because it was getting hotter and the adders might be coming out to sun themselves, back he'd come for breakfast – which, for some unknown Siamese reason, always had to be in his cage. By the end of the morning he'd be howling the valley down about how long he'd Been in There, had we Forgotten him, let him out at Once he was getting cramp... when we let him out, too, we always had such an exhibition of leg-stretching you'd think he'd been shut up in a matchbox instead of an enclosure the size of a room... but it was definitely the 'in' place for summer breakfast.

Charles said it was some sort of tabu; Seeley probably thought his whiskers would drop off if he ate breakfast anywhere else. My theory was that, subconsciously, it took him back to his ancestors' jungle days. He did some pretty peculiar things in it, anyway, which he never did in the house.

When he'd eaten his breakfast, for instance, he always camouflaged the saucer with moss and leaves and earth, raked up from the lawn with his claws. If he left a part of his food, he covered that in the same way. Once, given chicken out there as a treat, he covered it up so frantically without so much as tasting it that I thought he must be feeling off-colour. Apparently it was just that chicken wasn't a thing one ate in the cage, however, A while later, the rules overcome by peckishness, he scraped off the moss and leaves and scoffed the lot as if he hadn't eaten for a fortnight.

Was this inherited memory of what to do with his kill? Was the fact that, in his cage, he always burrowed under a rug to sleep a further mental throwback to his forebears? Indoors, or in the conservatory or the car, Seeley would sleep stretched out trustingly for all to see him. In the cage, however, though Sheba slept normally on top of the rug, a camouflaged bump beneath it was all one could see of Seeley. It wasn't to keep the draught out, either. He did it on the most sweltering of days.

All that had been in the summer, of course. In the winter, with no danger from adders, he'd come and gone as he liked while Sheba slept in front of the fire. But now it was April and adder time again and, as Charles still hadn't got round to building a permanent cage (Rome, as he was continually telling me, wasn't built in a day), one fine Sunday morning, when it was too nice for him to be indoors, into his temporary cage with his rug went Seeley.

I left Sheba in the conservatory, thinking it was a bit too early for her to sit in the open. And there I made my mistake, because while Seeley, if Sheba was with him, would stay happily in his cage all the morning, on his own he thought he was missing something and promptly proceeded to break out. The previous year he'd got out through all four top corners in turn, which was why we'd planned a stronger and permanent structure. Needs must when the devil drives the barrel-organ, however, as Charles is always saying, and so, as Charles was going off to fetch Aunt Ethel over for lunch and wasn't available for guard duty, Seeley went into the temporary cage while I got on with the cooking.

To say he protested would be an understatement. There were no little 'Woohs' and 'Mrr-mrrs' now.

Father Adams, plodding down the hill after his Sunday morning pint, said they could hear him up in the Rose and Crown. 'IT'S HIS FIRST TIME IN THE CAGE THIS YEAR,' I shouted above the uproar. 'HE'LL BE ALL RIGHT ONCE HE'S SETTLED DOWN.'

Eventually, indeed, there was peace. He was asleep under his rug, I decided, and was sure I could see the tell-tale bump. I didn't go out to check, not wanting to start him off again – and so, when I eventually did go over and discover the empty cage… with, in front of it, the tell-tale hole where he'd burrowed under the wire like a dog… I didn't know how long he'd been gone.

I could give a couple of dozen guesses as to what he was doing, however. Right at that moment about to pounce on an adder in the orchard… equally right at that moment being chased up the lane by some Sunday morning walker's dog… if he wasn't out on the road at the mercy of speeding motorists, or (the distance depending on how long since he'd got away), miles across the fields, heading fast for the coast and Siam.

As a matter of fact he was just across the lawn. He must have been there all the time but in my initial state of jet-propelled panic… up the lane, down the lane and a frenzied yodelling of 'Seeleyweeleyweeley' over the Forestry gate that set the pigeons flapping out of the trees like bats… I didn't think of his being close at hand.

He wasn't telling me, either. Enjoying, as Siamese do, the spectacle of people tearing round in search of them when they are there within earshot all the time, it was only as I came panting past from the back gate towards the front that I happened to glance at the conservatory doorway and saw him sitting framed in it like the *Mona*

Lisa, regarding me with the look of wide-eyed innocence that is known to every Siamese owner.

Was there a fire somewhere? his expression demanded. And who was I supposed to be calling? Hadn't I realised where he'd gone? He just wanted to be with Sheba.

After that we abandoned the idea of a permanent cage. It was more sheltered for Sheba in the conservatory, Seeley obviously preferred to be with her, all we had to do was make a wire door and window guards for when it was hot and the windows had to be opened – and there, under a jungle-like ceiling of grape leaves, they were happy in the hottest weather.

We had some hot days that summer, too. Often it was six o'clock before the sun cooled sufficiently to make it safe to let Seeley out, and even then I checked the hillside to make sure there was nothing about.

I thought I made sure, anyway. One night I did my usual perambulation, bashing round the bushes with a clock-golf club and talking loudly to Annabel as I went (that was so the adders could hear the vibrations of my voice; the procedure wasn't quite so batty as it looked). Then I let Seeley out of the conservatory and, following his usual motto of never being in the garden if he could be out of it, up he raced like a gazelle on to the hillside... and within seconds was racing back down off it again, carrying something in his mouth that was long and thin and squirming.

Actually it was a slow-worm. If it hadn't been I wouldn't have given much for his chances, the way its head was curling up around his face. I wouldn't have given much for mine, either, seeing that he laid it very lovingly right at my feet. Clever, wasn't he? he demanded, poking it to make it perform – and was obviously most put out when, holding it balanced across the clock-golf club, whence it kept falling off and having to be balanced again, I gingerly deposited it in a bramble bush.

The next night he went up and caught another one. This time, since I didn't appreciate his presents he didn't bring it down to me but sat prodding it playfully up on the hillside. As at that distance we still couldn't guarantee that it was only a slow-worm Charles immediately charged after him, armed with the garden hoe and yelling in the hope of scaring him off.

It was asking for it, of course. 'Whass he after then, Red Indians?' enquired Father Adams, appearing on the scene as if by magic. 'That liddle old cat can handle *snakes*,' he observed when I explained the situation. And then, shading his eyes to follow the fleeting Charles – 'Thy old man's going to fall down flat as a cow-dab runnin'– like that – thee'st see if he don't,' he announced.

For the record Charles didn't fall down – which was just as well since he had to repeat the performance many a night that summer – and Seeley couldn't handle snakes. He'd learned nothing from his adder bite of the previous year, when he d been bitten on his paw. He still poked at anything that wriggled, picked it up by its middle instead of the back of its head and, when he saw us running after him, dodged with it into the undergrowth.

As at the same time he had a genius for finding the things... case the hillside though I might, within minutes of his going up there he'd have fished one out from somewhere... and since, though at that time of night there shouldn't have been adders about, we could never be sure there weren't, we were constantly on the run.

We'd thought Solomon was bad enough about snakes. Seeley practically made them his life's work.

None of them was an adder, though, thanks to our keeping him in during the day. And eventually he ran out of slow-worms and turned, more prosaically, to mice. These at least he brought down to the cottage lawn. The dead ones we let him keep, the live ones we spirited away... and one day we saw something we never expected to see again. Sheba playing with a mouse.

She hadn't caught one in years. For ages she hadn't even been interested when Seeley caught one, turning her head with indifference when he started showing off. Recently, though, she'd been taking more notice of things. She must have seen us chasing after him on the hillside when he caught the slow-worms, for instance, and one day, instead of coming sedately indoors for her supper as she usually did, she vanished when we let the two of them out of the conservatory and gave us a considerable fright. We were afraid, when we couldn't find her anywhere in the cottage or the garden, that she might have gone quietly off somewhere to die. We knew that she was very old and ailing, and cats do sometimes go off like that.

Sheba hadn't. When, after scouring every corner we could think of, Charles climbed as a last resort up on to the hillside, there she was in Annabel's field sitting in the evening sun. She hadn't been up there for years and we could hardly believe our eyes. Sheba looked placidly back at us. Seeley went up there and we made a fuss of him... now she was doing it, she informed us with a squawk.

She began sitting in the lane by the Forestry gate, something else she hadn't done in years. She couldn't jump on to the gatepost now. She sat at its foot and we had to keep fetching her back again because of the danger from passing dogs. We were amazed, nevertheless, at this new determination. We were even more amazed, looking out of the window at breakfast time one morning, to see that where Seeley, a moment before, had been tossing a mouse around on the lawn – there, sniffing it with interest, was Sheba.

Even as we watched, she picked it up in her mouth. I regret to say that even as we watched, too, Seeley came dashing back, forgetful of his usual consideration for elderly ladies, and indignantly snatched it away from her. She got her mouse, though. A day or so later he brought home another one and I abstracted it while he wasn't looking. After some puzzled searching he went back to his hunting ground and I secretly gave the mouse to Sheba.

She was a young cat again as she snatched it up, gazed warily around her and triumphantly carried it into the conservatory. And there she, who hadn't eaten solid food for months and most of the time now we spoon-fed her, wolfed that mouse as if she were starving.

It wasn't, as we hoped, a return to health and strength for Sheba. Somehow she must have known she was near the end. She must have been going back over the things she'd so loved doing... mousing, sitting on summer evenings up in the field with Annabel, gazing up the valley from her lookout on the Forestry gate.

A week after the mouse incident she went up the garden one night with Charles for her usual walk and asked to be lifted on to the car bonnet There she made such a fuss of Charles, whom she'd always loved...

rubbing against him, purring, lifting her head to butt at his sleeve... that when he brought her down again he said she was like a kitten.

She didn't go out again. When we came down next morning she staggered as she tried to get up to greet us. There was nothing we could do for her. She'd had kidney trouble for years. Through the day she lay placidly curled in her rug. Through the evening we took it in turn to nurse her. Funny said Charles, to think of this time last night. She must have known, and she'd been saying goodbye to him...

She died the next day, as quietly as she had lived with us. It was sixteen years since she and Solomon had been born upstairs in the cottage. Now, with both of them gone, it seemed the end of an era.

Three

WE HAD LONG AGO decided that when we lost Sheba we would get another blue-point kitten as soon as possible. It wasn't callousness on our part. On the contrary it was because we were so fond of her. The place wouldn't seem right without a blue-point girl around it. Seeley had been the best cure for our grief when Solomon died. Seeley himself would be lost without a companion to Mrrr-mrrr his confidences to and sleep with... So we reasoned, and if occasionally the thought crossed my mind that the newcomer, when she materialised, might be a vastly different character from our placid, home-loving Sheba, I put it firmly from me.

It never worked like that, I told myself. I could think of lots of people who had a pair of cats and always one of them was a quiet one. Black and Blue from up the lane... Hardy and Willis, who'd once belonged to the Rector... Even with Sugar and Spice, the twin Siamese queens who lived with two schoolteacher sisters we knew, while Spice was an incorrigible delinquent with the mind of a Mephistopheles, the other one, Sugar, never gave them a moment's worry.

Since Seeley went from crisis to crisis with the inevitability of a James Bond serial it followed that the newcomer was bound to be like Sheba. She'd better be, anyway, if Charles and I were to survive.

Seeley had recently scared the daylights out of us by eating a rubber spider. Someone had sent it to him for Christmas and for months, suspended from the latch of the living room door, where it turned squeamish visitors quite queer when they saw it, it had been his favourite toy. He had played with it by the hour. Leaping at it with high-sprung Siamese leaps, growling at us over it with sinister Siamese growls, rushing across the room with it as far as the elastic would stretch and then letting it snap back, as deliberately as a boy with a catapult, to hit the door with a thump.

Then one night I cut down on his bedtime snack because he'd eaten so much during the day. He'd be getting far too fat, I told him reprovingly. He didn't want to be known as Tub-turn, did he? Apparently he did, because when I came down in the morning it was to find that he'd filled the gap with his spider. There was one small piece of it left on the hearthrug. The rest... the legs, the sinister-looking head, half the flabby black body and about a yard of elastic with a ring on it... was patently inside Seeley's stomach.

I nearly dropped when I thought of it. Visions filled my mind of his having to be operated on... just one bit of that rubber, as well I knew, could cause a fatal blockage if it stuck. I had an immediate further vision of the Vet missing one of the pieces (the spider's legs were so long and feathery and he'd probably chewed them all in shreds). Remorse overwhelmed me because I hadn't let him have those cat-biscuits; if I had, his little stomach wouldn't have been in jeopardy now.

I was trembling like a leaf as I made for the door to shout for Charles. I was still trembling when, spotting something odd lying by the door-jamb, I bent down to see what it was. And then I went quite weak-kneed with relief. There, neatly sicked up in a heap, were the missing spider parts. On top lay the ring and the elastic, which had presumably brought about their recall – and, looking at them, it was fortunate that they had. The ring was the size of a 10p piece. If that had gone down through Seeley's gullet, nothing short of surgery would have got it out again.

After Charles had checked the bits to make sure that none was missing... the things he had to do in this house, he said, it was a good thing his stomach was strong... we added another rule to our code for Siamese safety. Never to leave Seeley alone again with anything made of rubber and chewable, and to see that his toys were locked in the bureau at bedtime.

He still had plenty of ways of putting the years on us, however. The next day he went out and fell in the rain-water tank. It was a fine bright morning and we were having breakfast with the windows open when it happened, which was how we came to hear the rumbling noises, as of distant muffled thunder.

'Miss Wellington pushing her garden roller,' I commented to Charles. And then, as we debated why she should be trundling her roller around in the lane... she does some pretty odd things but we couldn't account for that one... I heard the rumbling again.

'Seeley's in the water-tank!' I yelled with sudden comprehension. And up we leapt like a couple of greyhounds... we may not have the staying power but quite a few Olympic runners would have a job to beat us at the take-off after our years of Siamese cat-keeping... and out into the garden, my mind ranging frantically while I ran as to what we could possibly *do* to get him out. Charles lowering me into it head-first by my heels seemed about the only possibility, since the eight-foot high tank was bolted to the wall, the water-level – being summer – was very low indeed, and Seeley, trapped as in a bear pit at the bottom, couldn't possibly, poor little chap, jump out.

That was what we thought. As we rounded the corner we met him marching across the lawn. 'It couldn't have been him in the tank,' I said. And then I saw the mud on him and his woebegone expression.

He must have been stalking birds on the garage roof. We'd spotted him up there several times incognito behind a branch of the plum tree. He'd presumably jumped at one; landed on the wire-netting which covered the tank for safety; his weight must have taken him, wire and all, down into the tank... initially he must have plunged into the foot of stagnant water at the bottom and then, scrambling onto the crumpled wire, he'd used it as a springboard to jump himself out. Even then he was lucky to have made it, with the wire sagging beneath him as he sprang. What would have happened if the tank had been half full of water and the wire hadn't been there for him to climb on, it turned us cold to think.

We pulled ourselves together, however. One has to, with Siamese cats. Charles got some planks for a temporary cover for the tank. I took our adventurer indoors and cleaned off the mud as best I could. And five minutes later, when I was telling a telephone caller what had happened... 'How on earth you two stay *sane*...,' she said. 'Oh, we take it all in our stride,' I demurred, with what I hoped was light-hearted nonchalance... Seeley decided it was time for the finale to the act. Coming out into the hall, so I shouldn't by any chance miss the performance, he crept pathetically to the foot of the stairs, sat down and began to heave. As I couldn't possibly put the phone down, either... or at least not fast enough to get to him in time – there I sat, trying hard to continue sounding nonchalant, while before my very eyes he sicked up mud all over an Indian rug. The only white one we had and why that horrible cat had to choose it...

So we'd realise what he'd Been Through, said Seeley, sitting fragilely by the side of the evidence. Gone right down into the Mud, he had. People who had Siamese cats ought to be careful how they Looked After them. Letting him eat that spider and now we'd let him fall in the tank...

We had another performance the day after Sheba died. She'd been such a negative companion to him in the last few months, I don't think as yet he'd really missed her. We'd taken him to bed with us that night, in any case, so he hadn't had to sleep alone. It was undoubtedly complete coincidence that he went off next morning and wasn't seen again for hours.

That wasn't the impression he gave Mrs Pursey, however. She and Farmer Pursey lived in a bungalow on the hill now, while their son and his wife I and small daughter lived along at the farm. And when she looked out of one of her windows and saw Seeley sitting in a flower-bed looking wistfully back at her, her heart went out to him in an instant.

She rang us up. She knew he shouldn't be so far away, she said, and that we'd be worrying about where he was. And when I thanked her and said I'd come straight up, I couldn't think why he'd gone up there... Perhaps he was missing Sheba, she said, and had come up to see her cat for company.

I doubted it. Possibly he'd followed Whisky up through the woods in the first place, but, having spotted somebody doing something inside a window, that was the great attraction. Seeley was just busy nosey-parkering.

I saw what she meant when I went up to fetch him, however. There he sat huddled under a dahlia. Scared to come out now he knew that he'd been spotted and with such a forlorn expression on his face one might well have taken him for a cat in mourning.

Couldn't think how he'd got up there, he assured me plaintively, riding on my shoulder down the hill. He'd just looked round and there he was... That lady was making a bed Downstairs, he commented, his voice becoming noticeably more confident the nearer we got to the cottage. Had I ever seen anybody do that? I loved him, didn't I? He rubbed his head against my face. He bet I was worried when I thought I'd let him get lost...

I certainly was. There I'd been panting round the district like a grampus... all the paths lead upwards out of the Valley and I'd kept coming hopefully back down to the cottage and having to climb up the hillside again...

And all the while, at the back of my mind, was the thought that we *couldn't* have lost him as well... not with Sheba only just gone from us... surely Fate wouldn't be so unkind as that...

She hadn't been. All the same, carrying him in and dumping him on the kitchen table, where he immediately started to complain to Charles about people not looking after him and he hadn't had his breakfast... 'We'd better get a kitten as soon as possible,' I said. 'She might help to keep him at home... and we ought to have two, just in case...'

So we set out on the search for Sheba's successor. We had no thought this time of getting a kitten that looked like her, as we'd done with Solomon. With him it had been possible. He'd been a seal-point and a typically handsome one at that. It had taken a month to find his double but at last we'd succeeded – with Seeley, who was so like Solomon he even had his spotted whiskers. But there weren't so many blue-points about and in any case Sheba hadn't been typical. She was pretty, but in a homely, round-faced sort of way. She'd never have been a prize-winner. We were never likely to find a kitten who looked like her and we knew it was a waste of time to try.

Prepared, nevertheless, to have to wait for weeks to get our new girl, what with blue-points being scarce and they were sure to be even more so when we wanted one, to our surprise we found her within a week.

My Aunt Louisa, watching the papers for us, rang us in great excitement with the advertisement. True she was so excited she'd mislaid her glasses, couldn't read the breeder's telephone number and hopefully gave us several combinations which she said might be the right one, but luck was with us. The first one we tried hit the jackpot.

Luck was with us again, too. We'd already answered one advertisement to find that the only female had gone. The rest of the little darlings, said their owner (there'd been a pause in the conversation at this point as, judging by the sound of it, she removed a little darling who'd been sitting on her head bawling his credentials down the receiver at me himself)... the rest of the little darlings – all five of them – were boys. Was I sure I wouldn't like a boy? she enquired hopefully. We already had one, I said sympathetically. We were looking for a girlfriend for him, to try to keep him at home.

The breeder I'd rung now had three blue-point girls, however. Three girls and a boy, she said. We were the first to ring and we could have our choice. Their father and grandfather were both Champions of Champions... Not to worry about that, I said. We were on our way.

Within an hour we were in town. It was just the background we'd hoped for. The loving home that produces a good-tempered Siamese (invariably egotistical, of course, but one can't have everything); the queen was the family pet, so that the kittens had been brought up in the house... they'd even let her have the kittens because they thought they'd be good for her psychologically, not with the idea of breeding for profit. Once in kitten she'd been given the best of food... properly balanced, too, since the breeder was a nurse... and there was the result, suddenly displayed before us, as Mrs Hinks opened the door and the kittens poured into the room.

I am a sucker for seal-points myself. The sight of one of those dark pansy faces, anywhere in the world, always stops me dead in my tracks with admiration. But there is something about a blue-point, too. An ethereal Ice Queen quality about their beauty... an impression of frosted moonlight on distant mountains... And when the four of them came tumbling in, I, as well as Charles, was lost.

There it was again. The old Siamese magic. The slanting, sapphire-blue eyes. The round little crew-cut heads. The lift of their little matchstick tails. The shrieks of joy with which they swarmed over the furniture, intent on making the most of what was obviously a special treat.

Mrs Hinks said it was. Normally, she said, they weren't allowed in the sitting room. They *would* go up the curtains and it didn't do them any good.

They were going up them now. Two were near the top, a third was close behind, a fourth – the boy, said Mrs Hinks – was halfway up, swinging busily upside down. Even as we watched he let go, turned a quick half somersault and landed on the back of the settee. That was how she knew it was the boy, said Mrs Hinks. He was the one who couldn't climb.

Even as we watched, too, the third one dropped deliberately off on top of him and the top two slid down from the heights as if they'd come down in a lift. In a moment it wasn't the curtains they were demolishing. It was the immaculate, linen-covered settee.

Siamese owners get used to this, of course. Over the years we'd gone through two sets of linen loose-covers ourselves and were now discovering the disadvantages, so far as Siamese are concerned, of the stretch variety as well. This was the breeder's first litter, however, and though she bravely tried to combat it, every one of those newly-pulled threads must have cut her to the heart.

'Well,' I said, scooping two of them off the back of the settee to help her out. 'They're lovely kittens. We're certainly going to have one of them. Which is it to be?'

It wasn't easy. It never is. To begin with, the boy kept being hauled out in the selection, up-ended and, to his indignation, rejected. Even when Mrs Hinks shut him outside the door, that didn't help things either. He started bawling under it about What Was Wrong With Boys? His sisters clustered interestedly on the inside all trying hard to see him underneath. It got them off the settee all right, but we could hardly choose a kitten by its bottom.

So we let him in again and the ballet began once more. Les Sylphides, I thought, struck by the fairy-like quality of their colouring. And then I noticed that one of the Sylphides kept stopping to sit in front of us, staring at us intently with that deep-seeing Siamese gaze. So, long ago, our first blue-point, Sugieh, had chosen us. Now another one had made up her mind that she was the one for us.

Four

WE PRETENDED SHE WASN'T at first. We checked the kittens for size; they were all about the same. We checked them for broad-headedness (Sheba had been broad-headed). Guess whose head, if anything, was just a fraction wider? We held them up one by one and studied them, trying to judge their intelligence. Guess who stared most seriously back at us, obviously judging ours?

So we brought her away with us. Worrying – there being always something – because she was only eight weeks old and hadn't been inoculated.

Once kittens were inoculated at six weeks. Now they have the new one-shot vaccine at ten weeks, usually while still with their mothers, and Siamese – the most vulnerable breed so far as feline gastro-enteritis is concerned – are rarely sold without a certificate of inoculation.

She'd wondered about that, said Mrs Hinks when we mentioned it. It was her first litter and she hadn't been sure what to do. But someone had told her people preferred to have the kittens at eight weeks old, to have the full fun of them, and it was only two weeks to wait and meanwhile the kittens, like human babies, would carry a natural immunity from their mother...

She spoke from her experience as a nurse. Whether Siamese cats followed the pattern was something we wouldn't have liked to bet on. They regard themselves as human when it suits them right enough, but when it doesn't there is nobody faster at assuming the role of fragile, fading flowers.

This, I might add, is not just the opinion of a besotted owner. Some catteries refuse to take Siamese, knowing their propensity for pining and picking up germs. Vets, too, have a wary regard for their temperaments. Take cat flu, as our own Vet once pointed out to us... not the feline gastro-enteritis that many people wrongly call cat flu, but the runny pulmonary variety. Other cats, he said, would sneeze and snuffle for a couple of days and then be as right as rain. Let a Siamese go down with it, however, and not only could the cat be really very ill but, if it felt so inclined, it would just give up the will to live and nothing on earth could save it.

I told this doleful tale to Mrs Hinks. Would we like her to keep the kitten for us, then? she said. She'd be perfectly happy to keep it another fortnight and have the inoculation done by her Vet.

But by this time, however, I'd thought up another snag. So far we were the first people to have seen the kittens. If we took one home with us now we knew it couldn't have been in contact with any infection.

Supposing we waited the fortnight, and in the meantime someone came to see them bringing some virus or other?

That, and the fact that having seen them we couldn't bring ourselves to go home without one – not with Seeley waiting for a companion, we said, though really of course it was for us – decided us.

Mrs Hinks rang their Vet to make sure. Quite all right with kittens as fit as theirs, he said... just so long as we had her done without delay at the end of the fortnight. We rang our own Vet to make even more sure. Quite all right, he confirmed encouragingly. He'd book us in for a fortnight's time if we liked.

So we brought her home. Still not completely convinced she'd survive the fortnight unprotected. Even less convinced when we saw the smallness of her in her basket. Certain of one thing only – that when Seeley saw her he was going to be the happiest Siamese in the country.

Which just showed how wrong we could be because when we took her into the cottage, let Seeley into the living room and opened the basket, fondly anticipating something like the balcony scene from Romeo and Juliet, Romeo put his ears down flat and said she was absolutely Horrible while Juliet, all five indignant inches of her, bushed her tail and crossed her eyes and said he was Horrible back.

He'd Eat her if she didn't go away, bawled Romeo. Just let him Try it, retorted Juliet, squaring up to him like a country batsman awaiting the village fast bowler. And that, it was patently obvious, was the end of our plans for getting them together that night.

We took Seeley to bed with us instead, leaving the new arrival downstairs with a rug and hotwater bottle on the settee. She followed us to the door when we went out and it wrung our hearts to close it on her, yet what could we do in the circumstances? Certainly we couldn't leave Seeley down there thinking we didn't want *him*.

Did I think she'd find her way back to her bed? asked Charles, lying awake in the darkness and worrying about her. Of course she would; she'd be crying if she couldn't, I said. My own worries revolved around that non-inoculation.

But she hadn't gone back to the settee. Just inside the living room door, on the bottom shelf of the Welsh dresser, was a polystyrene tile which Charles, who is fond of painting, had been experimentally using as a lightweight palette. And on that, curled up in the middle of the paint pans like a little mink ball on a plate, we found her asleep in the morning.

She couldn't have done more to win Charles's heart if she'd gone out into a snowstorm wearing a shawl. Gosh, she was a brave little thing, he said. Tucking herself up like that, as near to us as she could get. And she hadn't cried *once*... that showed what spunk she had. Did I realise how intelligent she was, too, to have discovered that polystyrene was warm instead of sleeping on the wood of the dresser?

I lifted my eyes heavenwards and went out to get breakfast and Seeley, raising his tail at an angle that obviously expressed the same sentiment, departed for his walk. We were welcome to her, he said.

The saving grace about the next few days was that, being summer, Seeley still followed his conservatory routine. Giving her a snarl like a Bengal tiger as he passed through the living room first thing in the morning, just to show her who was who about the place, he then forgot about her for the rest of the day. He had his walk, breakfasted in the conservatory, took his siesta beneath the vine leaves as he'd always done with Sheba. When I let him out later, too, there was no suspicious rushing indoors to see if she'd gone. He'd go up into the orchard to talk with Charles or entice me up to play with him on the hillside, diving exuberantly into the clumps of dried grass and charging up successions of trees as though kittens just didn't exist. Only when evening fell and he came back into the cottage did the cloud of her presence descend upon him. And then – 'TCHAAAH!' he would spit, like a lorry-driver releasing his air-brakes, and go and sit disgustedly on the table.

He sat there for four nights following like a sailor on a raft in a sea of sharks. Right in the middle, in case he fell off, and barricaded, for extra safety, behind a transistor radio and a wooden candelabra. To give him confidence I used to arrange his defence works for him and there he crouched, like a settler besieged by Indians, occasionally peering over the stockade to see what the enemy was doing.

It might have helped had the enemy been interested in him – as, when he was small, he'd been so persistent in his pursuit of Sheba. This one, however, was made of different stuff. Pausing only to arch her back like an inch-worm when she caught him peering at her... she didn't bother to spit at him now; it obviously frightened him a whole lot more when she did such things in silence... she played and scampered and ate at ground level as if he didn't exist.

It was the eating that finally began the breakthrough. We'd thought Seeley had a big enough appetite, but Shebalu, as we'd decided to call her... Sheba for old times' sake and Lu in honour of Louisa who'd found her for us... Shebalu, despite her breeding, ate like Oliver Twist. 'Nmmm-nmmm-nmmm-nmmm' she hummed as she gobbled through her food and Seeley, creeping cautiously to the edge of the table on the second night (on account of as yet the enemy hadn't attacked) could hardly believe his eyes.

She *couldn't* hold that much, he wailed incredulously... retreating hastily behind the transistor as she paused in her eating to look up at him. Not only did she hold it, however. When she'd finished she went out to the kitchen and brought in the dishmop by way of a savoury course.

She'd discovered it during the day. I'd already taken it back about a dozen times and the sight of her determinedly dragging it in again was by this time part of the scenery. Not for Seeley, however, who'd been absent in the conservatory, and when she appeared stumbling along with the mop-handle between her legs like a miniature hobby-horse he so far forgot himself as to get down off the table for a closer look. Neck extended, eyes like organ stops, he watched from behind a chair as she sat down and began to chew it. Then I took it away from her and he departed once more for his raft.

It was a start, however. He ventured more and more often to the edge of the table. The third night he actually got down twice and looked at her from behind the coal-scuttle. Even so it was a far slower process than his get-together with Sheba had been and on the fourth night, exasperated by his eternal peering round chairs as if gremlins were after his toes, I decided to put an end to it.

I built him a newspaper hide – something which Seeley, with his love of thinking himself invisible, has never been able to resist. He couldn't resist it now. He got inside, crouched, and watched, as he thought, unseen. In a moment up pranced Shebalu and poked in an inquisitive blue paw. And, after a pause long enough to think out a dozen chess-moves, out came a cautious, very large black one. The moment she touched it he leapt as if he'd been stung, of course, but that was just reaction. Within no time they were taking it in turn to hide in the paper while the other one, highly excited, dodged and threatened outside.

It wouldn't have worked had we tried it the first night. Probably the success of it, even now, lay in the fact that they were playing in anonymity, without actually seeing each other. And after a while they forgot about staying under cover, and eventually Seeley gave Shebalu a lick... a very shamefaced one; obviously it was much beneath his dignity; but he shut his eyes and pretended it wasn't him... and there we were. Mission accomplished.

We still had to be careful, of course. Not to make a fuss of her when he was around, in case it made him jealous. Not to let them eat together, otherwise she cleared her plate at the double and then started in on his. The odd thing was that he let her. Until Sheba's death he had

been the extrovert... young, exuberant, avid, grabbing all
the food in sight without a thought for Sheba. And now,
within a week, here he was sitting paternally by while a
kitten tucked into his rabbit.

She was Little, he said, shutting his eyes at me when I
told him how silly he was. We had to look After her, he
added, moving back a couple of paces so she could get
at his plate more easily. And so, to preserve the balance,
we fed them separately. She in the hall, he in the living
room, and even then she only had to yell through the
door when she'd finished and he'd leave something on
his plate, quite obviously for her.

No doubt about it, he was a changed cat. The day after
their get-together Charles came in to report that he'd
actually seen Seeley spraying. Up in the Forestry lane
against a bramble, he said, with a determined look on
his face. Within no time, too, we saw him chasing the cat
from down the lane... not wandering affably after it as
he'd always done before but seeing it out of the garden,
quite obviously repelling invaders.

'He's woken up to the fact that he's got a girlfriend,'
said Charles. And though you'd hardly have thought she
was his girlfriend if you'd seen him playing with her…
flattening his ears, threatening to pounce and arching his
back... if you watched carefully you saw that his pounces
always missed; when he appeared to be locked in mortal
combat kicking the daylights out of her he was in fact
holding her in the gentlest of grips kicking industriously
into thin air; and that the only one who really contacted
was Shebalu who, with the determination of a black belt
Judo wrestler, hurled herself again and again at his great
dark back and head.

They progressed like a house on fire. All Siamese are individuals and in no time those two had evolved a play routine we had never seen in any of our cats before. I looked up entranced from my reading one night and signalled to Charles to watch. Quite oblivious of anybody looking on, they were silently performing a dance. They faced each other, as if it were a back-cloth, in front of a yellow-covered armchair. Seeley, ears back, his eyes on Shebalu, retreated several paces backwards and stopped. Shebalu, her ears sleeked back like a ballerina, walked the corresponding five paces forward and paused as well. Then, even as we watched, she went into reverse while Seeley advanced gracefully, sinuously, towards her... It was part, of course, of their eternal boisterous mock-fighting... one threatening, the other retreating, and then the positions being reversed... but it looked so much like a professional tango that we could almost hear the music as we watched it. And they kept it up for quite a while. And the next night they did it again.

I reckoned we could leave them together now, I said. So the next day, after Seeley had breakfasted in the conservatory, we put Shebalu in with him to see what happened. We kept an eye on her, of course. She polished his plate, looked out of all the windows, ate a spider she found in a corner and was promptly sick. And then she joined him in the armchair and when next I looked through the window he was lying on his side and she was perched on top of him. Looking smaller than ever, like a sparrow on a Trafalgar Square lion, and earnestly washing his ears.

There was no doubt as to who was in charge. After a while Seeley, tired of her ministrations, ducked his head and tried to dodge. Immediately out came a paw the size of a saltspoon, his head was held firmly in place in imitation of the way her Mum had dealt with her, and the washing continued. Neither did Seeley try to escape again; he closed his eyes and meekly submitted.

So, that night, we let them sleep together. There were no complaints from Seeley. No wailing about wanting to go to bed with us or bumping noisily around the room to get us up. When, wondering whether things were perhaps too silent, we checked on them at three in the morning, they were curled cosily together on the settee. Romeo and his Juliet, just as we'd envisaged them – as Solomon and Sheba had been through all their years together. Seeley was awake and watching us, of course. What buoyant young Siamese wouldn't, with a girl like that to guard?

We went happily back to bed ourselves and slept the sleep of the successful. Rather prematurely, unfortunately. Next morning Seeley left home.

Five

HE WAS MISSING FOR six hours. Longer than he'd ever been away in his life. To add to the tension his absence coincided with the baker knocking down our garden wall, though it was not until some time after the young man had departed... profuse in his apologies, explaining that he was new to the van and its brakes, hadn't realised the corner was so steep and, as he put it, "twere a good job the wall were there to stop'n, wun't it?'... that the thought occurred to us which resulted in our moving the pile of stones like frenzied navvies in case Seeley was underneath, my ringing the bakery to check that he hadn't gone off in the van, and my ringing them again, at Charles's insistence, to ask would they please look underneath in case he was on the axle.

He wasn't. On which happy note, with Charles convinced that he probably had been, but had fallen off in the road somewhere en route, I embarked on my usual search for him through the Valley and set off another sequence of events.

It so happened that it was a Wednesday and Ern Biggs was working up at the Upcott's cottage. Ern actually belonged to an adjoining village but some six months earlier one of our neighbours, Bill Trammell, meeting him in the pub and being impressed by Ern's own account of what a first-class gardener he was, had offered him a couple of mornings' work a week. This upset Father Adams, who, despite the fact that he couldn't possibly cope with it, considered that he should be asked to do all the odd-job gardening that was going, but that is by the way. Once having set spade in the village Ern found so many people wanting their gardens done that he'd introduced his brother Bert as well, and now there were two of them working in the district. As stolidly plodding as shire horses, pausing to size up Father Adams from under their hat brims whenever they saw him – while Father Adams, I regret to say, regarded them witheringly and spat.

Some people liked them, others didn't... the one thing people did agree on was that them Biggs brothers couldn't half *talk*. We'd had some of Ern ourselves. We didn't employ him, Charles preferring to do his own odd jobs even if they did take years in the doing – but that didn't stop Ern, on his way home from the Trammells, pausing to give us advice on rebuilding Annabel's house, spraying the fruit trees, or what he'd do if he was us with the vegetable garden. Advice which, illustrated with instances of what he'd recommended to other people in similar circumstances and they all now regarded Ern as the tops, was apt to last so long that we now took cover in the garage when we saw him coming. Particularly since he had somewhere learned that I made home-made wine and had been throwing out hints about wanting to try it.

When, therefore, I panted up the track above the wood, calling (Seeley-weeley-weeley' as hard as I could go and sweating on the top line because Charles had just reported seeing the retriever from down the lane trekking along that way and I didn't want the two of them meeting up, it didn't exactly help matters to see Ern up the lane ahead of me, methodically laying the Upcott's hedge with a billhook.

The one thing in my favour was that he was shortsighted. So am I, but not to the extent that he was. So I halted in my tracks, gazed vaguely about me and pretended that that was as far as I was going.

'Lookin' fer a dog?' called Ern.

'No,' I shouted back. 'A cat.'

'Gert black dog come through here just now. He belong to thee?'

'No,' I said. 'He's from down the lane.'

'Where d'ust thee live?' Ern peered at me myopically.

'Down in the Valley,' I said.

'Bist thee Mrs Trammell?'

'No.' I gazed around again. 'Well, I'd better be going. He obviously isn't up here.'

With which, filled with frustration because it was very likely that Seeley was further up the path but if I tried to pass Ern I'd be caught for the rest of the morning, back I came to report to Charles that I'd try the lane from the other end – which meant going uphill through the village, up another hill by the pub, and then back, full circle along the lane that Ern was in, only this time I'd be on the other side of him.

He *would* have to be in that blasted lane, I thought, scurrying up the first hill like the White Rabbit, thinking of all I might have been doing. Only, as I reached the top, to see a figure with a billhook ahead of me. Ern! I thought with dismay, recognising the trilby hat, the sack he always carried over his shoulder and the shambling, steel-tipped clump of his enormous boots. And how he'd got there so fast and where he was going... across the fields seemed the answer to the first question and to the pub the second, except that it wasn't yet opening time and he usually worked till midday.

The thing was, anyway, not to catch up with him. So, desperate by now as to where Seeley might be but I'd be sunk if I had to talk to Ern, I began to loiter. Not so easy in a village where one is known and to start lurking along the road intently studying the gateposts is apt to give the impression that one has gone bonkers. And Ern kept stopping to peer round to see who was behind him, at which I stopped too and gazed interestedly at the sky – and then, darn me, when he got to the Rose and Crown he didn't go in there after all, but turned to the left and trudged on up the slope.

This hill was even steeper. He stopped to look back so many times, and there was only one gate-way in which to loiter, that I threw discretion to the winds and openly hid in it, cocking an eye round the corner at him till he'd gone. Then, emerging from my hiding place – realising too late that Fred Ferry was watching me interestedly from over the hedge and a fine story that was going to make when he told it in the pub – I belted up the hill, turned into the lane, and once more started calling for Seeley.

There was no sign of him. But as I reached the point in the lane where it begins to dip to the Valley, I heard a whistle far below, from Charles. 'Has he come back?' I yelled at the top of my voice. There was no answer. Charles apparently couldn't hear me. Certain, however, that Seeley must have returned I let myself go in a ballet dance. It was a lovely day, Seeley was safe, Ern had gone home and the turf was so quiet and soft and springy, up there, high above the rest of the world. 'Dah... dah... dee-dah... dah' I sang, leaping with outstretched arms around the corner. And there, regarding me dourly from the spot where I'd seen him before, was Ern, complete with billhook, still in the process of trimming the hedge.

'I knows who thee bist,' he said. He ought to seeing that I'd just landed like a grasshopper right in front of him. I knew now, too, who it must have been going up the hillside ahead of me. His brother Bert, on his way home from some other job at the top of the village. He, too, wore a trilby and carried a sack, and at that distance I hadn't recognised him.

'Found thee dog?' asked Ern.

'Cat,' I said. 'Yes, he's come back home all right.'

'What be doin' up yer then?'

'Going back down to the Valley,' I said. (And that, I thought settled *him*.)

I was no match for Ern, however. In four quick moves – an enquiry as to where the pub was, though the wily old so-and-so knew as well as I did; an enquiry as to what time they opened, though that he probably knew even better; the comment that he wun't half thirsty... wun't it I as made thic home-made wine? – in four moves flat he had me.

'Come in on your way home and have a glass,' I said. And made my way back down to the cottage knowing that that was another hour's hold-up for sure and all on account of that blasted cat...

Who, I discovered when I got back, hadn't come home even yet. Charles said he'd been whistling to know if I'd found him. So Charles had the pleasure of serving Ern with his elderberry wine while I went on with the search, and all I got for that piece of hospitality was the conversation I heard – on account of the way sounds carry in the Valley – as I toiled up yet another hillside calling for Seeley.

'Whass she shoutin' for?'

'One of the cats,' said Charles.

'Thought she'd found 'un.'

'No, she hasn't,' said Charles.

'I seen she up in the top lane *dancin*'.' Ern's confidential tone showed what he thought of that.

'She often does,' said Charles. And that didn't help much, either.

The morning's score so far was a knocked-down wall, Seeley still missing, Fred Ferry and the brothers Biggs convinced that I was dotty – and we hadn't finished yet.

Charles, when he'd got rid of Ern, said it had occurred to him... the Trammells had been up outside their cottage with the car-boot open. He supposed Seeley couldn't have got shut in there?

Guess who was deputed to go and ask them to look in the car-boot. The Trammells hadn't been there long.

They knew me only as somebody eternally calling for a cat up and down the Valley – when, that was, I wasn't banging an enamel bowl to coax a donkey down from the heights. To be asked if they had our Siamese cat in their boot was hardly the best of introductions, but Charles was insistent, so I did it.

He wasn't there, of course. They pulled out the boot-rug and shook it, to make sure they'd convinced me. We never knew where he'd been. Only that he returned at two in the afternoon, having left at eight in the morning, as nonchalantly as if he'd been for a five-minute stroll round the garden. We could only think he'd been up all night watching Shebalu – to make sure she didn't eat him, not by way of looking after her – and that he'd gone off somewhere exhausted and had a darned good sleep.

We watched him carefully for the next few days, not wanting a repeat performance of his disappearance. We might as well not have bothered, of course. There was this new habit of his of chasing the cat from down the lane. One morning he was sitting by the fishpond while I was doing some gardening, the other cat passed the gate, and whooosh! Seeley was through the bars at a bound, chasing him up the hill. I whooshed after him, too. I might even have caught him – I was shouting so hard, not wanting him to vanish, that for a second he hesitated and looked back. At which moment a gun went off, I jumped yards and both cats shot into the wood and straight up a sycamore tree.

It wasn't anyone after us. It was another newish neighbour practising shooting at a tin. I didn't know him very well, either – certainly not enough to say would he mind not firing his gun, our cat had gone up a tree. So there I stood. Afraid to move in case the marksman saw the branches waving and mistook the cats for pigeons. Calling Seeley frantically whenever the firing stopped, when a worried little face would appear in the fork above me. And then the gun would go off again, and Seeley would promptly vanish.

We'd have been there still if Charles, spotting what had happened, hadn't come staggering up the hill with the extending ladder. We'd have been there still trying to hoist it up into the sycamore, too, if a friend hadn't come along and discovered us in our predicament. He was on his way down to us with a home-grown cucumber which he laid carefully on the edge of the road, climbed the bank and helped us thread the ladder up through the tree.

The target practice had stopped by this time. The marksman, across on his patio, was more intrigued by watching us. We now had another snag, however, in that while Seeley kept appearing in the fork and peering down at us, the other cat kept appearing behind him as well – at which Seeley left off to chase him back to the end of the branch, and we were back once more where we started.

It was at this point, with the three of us holding the ladder in the air, gazing anxiously upwards and apparently waiting for Jacob to descend, that Ern Biggs plodded past on his way home from the Trammells.

'Whass they doin' then?' he asked the man with the gun.

'Blowed if I know' came the answer.

'Reckon they'm pickin' they?' said Ern, spotting the cucumber by the roadside. And then... I knew it was coming... 'I seed she dancin' up in the lane the other day,' he ventured in his confidential voice.

We effected the rescue eventually. Charles climbed the ladder, coaxed Seeley on to his shoulder and descended to a level where I could lift him off. I was the first to come out of the wood – sliding down the bank on my bottom, holding Seeley over my shoulder by his tail and, when I reached the road, getting up with as much dignity as I could and marching down the hill towards the cottage. Next came the other cat. Once Seeley was out of the way he shinned down of his own accord. And finally, slithering down the bank with the ladder, picking up the cucumber and looking remarkably, like Laurel and Hardy, came Charles and our helpful neighbour.

'Rum lot thee'st got round here,' Ern's voice floated after us complacently. 'Never knows what thee'st goin' to see.'

We, for our part, were glad that as yet we only had one cat to run after. Until her inoculation we were keeping Shebalu indoors. We dared not think what might happen when she was at large as well. She was, as we were daily discovering, very different from Sheba.

Six

SHEBA HAD BEEN A good girl. Demure; a trifle prim, perhaps; never had she given us a moment's worry. True in her old age she'd become a bit of an autocrat, but what old lady doesn't? Like Queen Victoria in her eighties was Sheba and one thing we knew for certain. Even in her giddiest days she'd never have drunk the dishwater.

Shebalu did. She also licked the sink and, when I'd been using the grillpan, could invariably be found wherever I'd left it, rasping away at the grid. She had the manners of an alley-cat, not the daughter of a Champion of Champions.

Terrible, wasn't she? enquired Seeley, who seemed to have grown up overnight since her coming and spent a lot of his time sitting anxiously by her looking like a furry paternal owl. Why did I let her *get* at the dishwater? said Charles, who worried in case it upset her stomach.

The answer was that I couldn't stop her. Most people pour dishwater down the sink, but if we did, it blocked the drains. Something to do with the pipes not being sloped enough, which Father Adams said wun't surprising seeing the builder that laid 'em. The fact was, anyway, that by long-established custom I threw the greasier dishwater either into the stream or on the garden. Not wishing to be seen doing this (people thought I was odd enough without adding compulsive water-throwing to my list of peculiarities), I was in the habit of peering through the doorway to see if anyone was about and, if there was, leaving the bowl in the sink until the coast was clear. This was when Shebalu got at it.

To avoid this I started dodging out with the bowl much more quickly and – my mind being more on dumping the dishwater than on the actual washing-up – embarked on a period in which I was constantly heaving teaspoons over the wall. I'd done this before in moments of stress. Over the years Father Adams had many a time and oft appeared with one of our teaspoons saying he'd found he in the stream and what was I narked with the Boss about this time, then? Now they were going over practically in shoals. I didn't see them when I threw them, of course, owing to the murkiness of the dishwater. But several times I found them laid by unknown rescuers on the gatepost; Father Adams, when he returned one now, handed it in resignedly and never said a word; and inevitably, in due course, Ern Biggs clumped in, importantly bearing a trophy.

'Found he in the stream on me way home from Mr Trammell's,' he said.

'Oh – many thanks,' said Charles. 'My wife throws them over the wall. When she gets flustered on account of the cats,' he hurriedly explained.

'*Do* she now,' said Ern.

Was it my fancy or from then on did we have more visitors to the Valley than ever? Customers from the pub coming down, thanks to Ern, in the hope of seeing me throwing teaspoons?

If so they were disappointed. After the episode with Ern I was a lot more careful with the dishwater. As Shebalu wasn't allowed out she couldn't cause any trouble. The only thing of consequence for quite a while was the disappearance of Seeley's golf balls and a passer-by would scarcely have noticed that.

I hardly noticed it myself to begin with. The first time I looked for the ball where I thought I'd left it – on the lawn by the clock golf hole – I decided I must have been dreaming. Must have taken it back to the kitchen, I thought, and went to fetch another one. The next time I wasn't dreaming, however I *knew* I'd left it by the hole. A timely putt with that, when Seeley was in a wandering mood, often diverted him from going off into the woods – but it had to be ready for the emergency; it was no good having it stowed away indoors.

I looked down the hole. It wasn't in there. I thought of magpies... it was a bit too heavy for them. I looked at Seeley, who regarded me owlishly back. No. Big as he was, even he couldn't have swallowed it.

So I reasoned – and several balls later (a present to him from a friend who'd given up golf) I was keeping a watchful eye on some children who were going past when I saw Nero, the black retriever, roaming around in the garden.

When I went out to chase him off he nipped through the hole in the wall made by the baker – obviously the way by which he'd come – and stopped in the lane to bark at me. A defiant, head-raised tirade with his legs spread stiff in challenge. Then he paused for a moment and I saw a bulge change places in his cheek.

'He's got Seeley's golf ball,' I said.

'He couldn't have,' said Charles. 'How could he manage to bark?'

He had it all right – though, realising his mistake, he didn't move the bulge again. He had a whole cache of our golf balls at home, hidden in the folds of his blanket. She'd been wondering where he'd been getting them, said his owner when I reported him; she hadn't known we had a clock golf course. Being another newcomer in the district I don't suppose that she did. Or – she looked a bit old-fashioned when I told her – that it was mainly used by one of our Siamese cats.

Anyway, Seeley got his golf balls back, the garden wall was rebuilt and Nero, to show what he thought of us for telling on him, took to barking whenever he saw us. A state of affairs that annoyed Seeley to the extent that one day – filled, we could only imagine, with the he-man image of himself which he'd acquired since the coming of Shebalu – he got deliberately through the bars of the gate and advanced for a confrontation.

They met, it being refuse collection day, by the dustbins on the corner.

Who, demanded Seeley, sticking his neck out and walking as stifflegged as a Texan gunfighter, did old Fancypants think he was, disturbing the district like that?

'Rooo-oooff' said Nero, doing a flop-footed bounce meant to frighten the daylights out of Seeley.

'Wanna fight?' enquired Seeley, adopting his combatant's stance. This, involving lowering his head till he was practically standing on it, bushing his tail and then advancing sideways like a crab, always worked wonders with the cat from down the lane. I don't really think it worked with Nero. I think it was more my nipping through the gate waving the broom I'd grabbed from the coalhouse. But when Nero turned and fled and Seeley went bounding after him, another legend was born in the Valley. Both Seeley and the people who saw him thought he must be a terror with the dogs.

It was a good thing Shebalu wasn't in on this lark, said Charles a day or two later, when, for the umpteenth time, we'd fetched Seeley back from a victory parade down Nero's lane. It was indeed. If Shebalu had been out not only would she have been parading with him; it was already quite on the cards that she'd have been in the lead.

There was no doubt as to who was going to be boss in this outfit. Less than a week with us and she could already open all the doors for a start. With the aplomb of a practised safebreaker she stood against the ones that pushed, pulled determinedly at the others with a midget paw till she forced a crack through which she could squirm – and jauntily in her wake inevitably came Seeley, taking it for granted that that was what girls were for.

This of course was because Sheba had always opened doors for him. He was a lot more perturbed when he discovered that Shebalu could climb. We happened to look through the conservatory window one day to check on them and there he was sitting in the chair, gazing upwards as incredulously as if she'd taken off for the moon to where, high up under the conservatory roof, she was balance-walking along a branch of the grapevine. She paused, graceful as a cheetah in a baobab tree, to look down at us through the vine leaves. Shouldn't be up there, should she? said Seeley. He was a silly old worrypants, said Shebalu airily.

He was also, like Solomon before him, an inveterate non-climber. Three feet up a fir tree, at the end of which he fell off, and Seeley thought he'd gone up Everest. His major trick until now had been to rush into the bathroom, heave himself laboriously up a coat behind the door and dangle from the top till he was rescued. Very much what Solomon used to do – except that Solomon at least used to make it to the top, and when he got there immediately bawled for help. Our only intimation of Seeley's predicament was a rush, a bump, and an ominous silence – at which combination we had to run like mad knowing that he was now hanging from the door by his paws, his nose over the top like Chad, far too scared to shout and his eyes round as an owl's with apprehension. He did this on average once a day and when we'd gone through the accepted routine of rescuing him – I lifted his front legs, Charles raised his back ones, and we hoisted him sideways off the door like a croquet hoop – he then went round as if he'd just been voted Sportsman of the Year.

After the business of Shebalu and the grapevine you'd have thought he'd let his climbing efforts sink into oblivion. But no. Convinced – after all he *was* born under Leo – that he was the greatest, and anxious to appraise everybody else of the fact, he now showed off his prowess even more. She climbed the grapevine during the day, he went up the bathroom door at night... On one occasion when we had visitors he went up four times in the course of the evening. Each time, at the sound of the bumps and thumps, we leapt like startled gamebirds and rushed hotfoot to the rescue. Our visitors were people who didn't know about Siamese cats. Why did he go up there if he couldn't get down again? they asked. When we said it was to substantiate his ego they looked at us as if we were mad.

If Seeley was Leo the Lion, however, Shebalu was Taurus the Bull – as well we knew when at breakfast time, with Seeley off for his walk, we locked her in the hall so that we could eat in peace.

She, as Seeley wasn't with her, imagined that he must be in with us. Eating. At the very thought of it she howled and roared and hammered at the door till, heavy though it was, it rattled. Whether she battered it with her head or her paws we didn't know. Only that we'd never had a kitten do that before (Seeley in similar circumstances had merely removed the draught excluder); that it was like the sound effects from Tannhauser while it lasted; and that when finally the thunder stopped there would be a pause (was she all right? we wondered); a nattering scamper up the stairs that proved she was; and finally a lot more thumping about in the bedroom as Taurus the Bull charged everything in sight, no doubt pretending it was us.

We laughed indulgently, pleased to hear such bounding high spirits. Until I went up one day and discovered

Taurus the Bull jumping off the spare room tallboy into a stack of glycerined beech-leaves. I was preparing them for a bazaar. The Committee had provided the glycerine. I was responsible for the entire supply of beech-leaves for sale on the stall. And at the sight of that horrible little cat jumping deliberately off into the middle of them... then out, up the tallboy and down into the middle of them... Honestly, I said. I just Despaired.

I despaired even more when I found the number there were with bent tops and the leaves riddled with teethmarks like bullet-holes. She must have been jumping into them for days. I stored them in the roof after that. A tardy closing of the stable door, of course. Not only did they look pretty motheaten when it came to putting them on the stall... Had I perhaps picked them a little too late? enquired one of the ladies... They seemed to have been got at by leaf-weevil... But Shebalu had now acquired a taste for plants.

I could hardly believe it when I found the clematis cutting I'd been cherishing nipped clean off in its prime. I thought a snail must have got it till I saw her later sitting in the window with her eyes closed, eating what was left of the stem as delicately as if it were asparagus. I could hardly believe it either when I found a rosemary cutting lying uprooted by the side of its pot – until, having re-planted it, I saw her pull it out again.

Charles said she probably wanted grass. She didn't, of course. I brought a large clump in and put it in a bulb-bowl for her but she took no notice of that. Wasn't *going* to look, she said, when I tried to show it to her. Plant-eating, it was obvious, was going to be Sheba's thing. Just as ripping holes in the staircarpet had been Solomon's, stripping the hide off a saddleback chair in the hall had been Sheba's, and whizzing round the bottom of another armchair on his back was Seeley's. Combined, in his case, with going up the bathroom door.

It would be better when she could go out into the garden, defended Charles. Meanwhile it looked as if locusts had attacked our pot-plants, the dish-mop lived perpetually on the living room hearthrug, and, trotting happily about the cottage when she wasn't doing any of these things, was a kitten apparently disguised as Father Christmas.

She'd adopted as her favourite toy a lambswool ball with a bell on it which had once belonged to Seeley. As we were fast discovering, she never did anything by halves. While he had been content to toss it around occasionally, and on odd occasions when he was being a Lion with his Capture, to carry it in his mouth across the room, you'd think it was fixed to her with glue.

She took it to the door to meet the milkman; into the bathroom, if the door was open, to talk to Charles while he shaved; she met every visitor with her ball in her mouth – or, if she missed out on their arrival, appeared carrying it, with the natural-born showmanship of the Siamese, at what she judged to be the most effective moment.

'Isn't she sweet?' they would exclaim as, tail raised, eyes crossed with willing them to look at her and apparently wearing a large white chin-beard, she advanced towards them across as vast an expanse of carpet as she could possibly contrive.

Which was all very well but there was a bell attached to that ball. And pretty though it sounded in visitor-sized doses – like dear little Japanese windbells, said Miss

Wellington listening to it nostalgically – when one had to live with it, it was more like Chinese torture.

From morning till night it tinkled. Sometimes faint, sometimes loud, according to where she was on the premises. Just a pause while she ate or slept, then the tinkling would start up again. It accompanied her to the Vet's when, at the end of the fortnight, she went bravely for her inoculation. It accompanied her a few weeks later to Low Knap when, while we were in Cornwall, she and Seeley went to board with Dr and Mrs Francis...

That itself was an indication of how things were turning out. We put her, for travelling, with Seeley in his big, wire-fronted basket. It would help to give her confidence, we said. She'd never been so far before. In fact it was she who bolstered up Seeley. While he crouched miserably in the basket as if he were in a tumbril, she sat perkily upright by his side as if she were doing the driving. While he wailed plaintively about Feeling Car-Sick whenever we looked back over our shoulders at him, she, peering out of the window, was positively entranced. And when we eventually arrived at Low Knap, Seeley, who'd been there before with Sheba, said the cat in the next enclosure was looking at him and please could we take him home... while Shebalu, now fourteen weeks old, emerged from the basket with the air of a Princess, formally inspected the chalet, went back into the basket to fetch her ball, which she took in and put in a corner...

We could go now if we liked, she said. She would look after Seeley.

Seven

THERE WAS NO NEED for that. He soon remembered where he was. When we rang that night to check on them the report was that he was busy eating his supper while Shebalu – she had finished hers, said Mrs Francis – was happily playing with her bell. When we went to fetch them four weeks later the Siamese next door was sitting like the Statue of Liberty on top of the tree-trunk scratching post in his run; Seeley – he was definitely Higher, he said – was sitting competitively on the post in his; and Shebalu, oblivious of either of them, was still playing with her bell. Our cats had been very good and they'd miss them, said Dr Francis, but as for that blasted bell...

We knew exactly what he meant. It rang all the way home, too. Though on that occasion, after four weeks without them, it sounded like heavenly music in our ears.

With the holidays over, however, now came the moment of truth. Eighteen weeks old and raring to go, we couldn't keep Shebalu in any longer. And, said Charles, we were going to have to watch her like a hawk, with all these gun-minded neighbours about.

Nobody would have potted at her deliberately, of course, but there was the man up the hill who practised with tin cans; our neighbour down the lane who liked pigeons en casserole for supper; John Hazell up at the top who occasionally tried out his .22. And, if we didn't keep an eye on her, there'd now be a little white kitten shinning up all the trees, looking, at a distance, like a plump young pigeon herself.

It turned me cold to think of it. Earlier that summer I'd had quite a scare myself. We'd been going off for a picnic. Charles was getting the car out, I was carrying up the supplies – I was just rounding the corner of the cottage with the picnic basket when shots hit the roof over my head. Some pieces of tile fell down, a couple of starlings emerged swearing from under the eaves and took off for safer climes and I... 'What's going ON!' I yelled indignantly, and wondered if I should take cover. It was the time of the Parish Council election. I was one of the candidates. Surely it couldn't be one of my rivals...

Deciding that it was probably somebody shooting pigeons... keeping a wary eye open nevertheless in case we *had* gone all Wild West... I shouted loudly for Charles and made for the Forestry gate. There was nobody there. Just drowsy summer silence and a soundless, dusty lane. As I ventured cautiously up the track a few feathers came floating down like snowflakes from overhead. But no marksman... and, if it came to that, no pigeon anywhere in sight.

'Old Sam from down the lane,' said Charles. Sam being the owner of Nero, an enthusiastic shot and, having been raised in the Australian outback, not very used as yet to living in confined English spaces. Intending to give him a piece of my mind, still clutching the picnic basket, I marched vengefully down the lane to Sam's... but there was no Sam either. Just complete and utter silence. The house lay sleeping in the morning sunshine. A couple of sulphur butterflies fluttered over a lavender bush. No sign of Nero anywhere and that in itself was something. He always bounced out as if he was on springs in exuberant defence of his home.

Charles, insisting on me staying indoors, now searched the other lanes. There was nobody there, either. We went for our picnic still wondering.

We wondered wrongly, of course. It was weeks later that Sam confessed that it had been he who'd fired the shot. Out of his bedroom window, which made an admirable hide for pigeons, he said. And when he'd heard me shout it made an admirable hide for him, too – realising I was all right, of course, he hastily assured me. Not knowing us very well at the time he'd shut the window, warned Nero not to bark and laid discretionally low. Was he forgiven? he asked.

He was, though he hadn't half caused us a mystery. Minded he of when he were a lad, said Father Adams when he heard the story... Over Belton way he used to live then, in a row of labourers' cottages. An' in the next village – Whittle 'twas called, where they had the limestone quarries – some of the miners used to keep racing pigeons and fly 'em on Sunday mornings. Many a time, said Father Adams, his eyes misting at the thought of his tender childhood, he'd been set to watch for the pigeons coming over and to tell his Dad when they did.

'He didn't...' I said incredulously. He did, said Father Adams. The blokes in Belton fair hated the Whittle lot. Many a Sunday dinner they'd had like that. Used to stand in their porches and take potshots when the Whittle birds come over. And when the copper came pantin' up, on about disturbin' the Sabbath, the guns was up the chimney and the blokes all busy diggin' their gardens... Hoping it wouldn't put ideas into his head – all we needed was Father Adams shooting out of his bedroom window as well – one night we thought it had. We were having supper when, from out in the lane, a gun went off like a thunderclap. The cats were in, Annabel was safely stabled... after a moment's pause with forks half-raised to our mouths we unfroze and went on eating. Some ten minutes later the gun went off again. This time I upset the coffee. And later on while I was washing up – so much later that I'd given up listening for further shots... Wham! Wham! went the shotgun again and I nearly went through the ceiling.

'The silly old fool,' said Charles, preparing to go out and tell Father Adams what he thought of him... we knew it wasn't Sam this time; he was away on business... At which moment, to complete the wrecking of my nerves, the telephone shrilled like an alarm clock.

It was John Hazell from up the lane. Had we heard those shots? he demanded hotly. Without waiting for a reply – John, when roused, strongly resembles a charging Highland bull – it was those damfool Biggs brothers, he said. Shooting pigeons along at the Trammells. Kept waking up the baby and making Janet jump. He'd had enough of it and he was going out to fire back.

'Now listen, John,' began Charles in agitation.

'Not at them, mon!' said John in his rich Scots voice. 'I'll be firm' at the old limekiln, just to gie' 'em a taste o' what it's like... I thocht I'd tell ye so ye won't imagine war has broken out.'

It was just as well he did warn us. Wham! a few minutes later went the Biggs' brothers' echoing shotgun. Wheeee! like a fast-winging bird, came John's gun in reply. And Whooooosh! (we weren't expecting that one) went a car up the hill within seconds, with Bert Biggs, white-faced, at the wheel and Ern crouched low beside him.

Stopping at the Rose and Crown for succour, and with Father Adams an ecstatic listener, they sweatingly told their story. Mr Trammell'd got pigeon trouble, reported Bert. Eatin' his sprouts, they was, confirmed Ern. So Bert had brought his gun... Mr Trammell'd said they could... and there they was, bangin' peacefully away in the lane, when this other bloke opened up.

'Bloody maniac whoever he was,' said Ern, his glass trembling like a jelly at the thought of it.

'Only just missed I,' said Bert – which was quite untrue but countrymen like their excitement.

'Hard luck, that,' said Father Adams ambiguously, his eyes raised innocently heavenwards.

The Biggs brothers didn't bring their gun again. All the same, with so many new folk about and this craze for random shooting being apparently catching, it was obviously politic to keep an eye on Shebalu, whom we envisaged trekking into firing range at every opportunity.

In point of fact not only did she, for weeks when we first let her out, stay happily on the lawn, but, to our amazement, Seeley solicitously stayed with her. We could leave them for minutes at a time – and when we went out there she'd be, as prominent as a snowdrop in a winter garden. Chewing off the grape-hyacinth leaves most likely, or busily demolishing the lavender – but always there, where we couldn't possibly miss her. And by her, wearing a look of doting benevolence, would be Seeley – or, if he happened to be out of sight (having decided, like us, that it was all right to leave her for a moment), even then he'd be no further than the vegetable garden, from which, if we came out and spoke to her, he'd come hurrying, full of anxiety and nattered Mrrr-mrrrs, to assure himself that all was well.

Only once he took her into the lane. To introduce her to Annabel presumably, because when I went tearing out to look for them, there they were across the track, peering in through the stable bars.

'In,' I ordered sternly – and Seeley, who'd learnt that command when young, belted guiltily back across the lane and over the garden wall. 'In!' I ordered Shebalu and, desirous of doing everything that Seeley did, she too dashed across the lane, leapt into the air – obviously without a clue as to why he'd done it but just because he had – and came down plop in the stream. Didn't Matter, she said, scrambling valiantly out. But that Seeley certainly did some funny things...

Apparently it was a favourite crossing place just there. A night or so later we happened to be going out. I was sitting in the car with the headlights on, while Charles closed the cottage gates, when suddenly across the lane in front of the car sped a fieldmouse going like a racehorse. Returning from sharing Annabel's supper, most likely, and obviously late for some other appointment. At the spot from which the cats had jumped, he took off into the air.

Up, across the stream and, with his stomach glinting silver in the headlights, straight as a well-aimed dart into a tiny hole in the wall. The ditch is a good three feet across. It was a clever jump for a mouse. I hoped the cats wouldn't spot that he as there, I said, and Charles said he was sure that they wouldn't. A mouse with enough sense to have a moat around his home, he said, was more than a match for cats.

So there we were. Back from our holidays, the snake season pretty well over, Shebalu apparently happy to stay in the garden and Seeley (we could hardly believe it) happy to stay in with her as well... At which otherwise peaceful point in our existence Miss Wellington noticed the dog lady.

We didn't know her name. Only that she came past the cottage occasionally with four or five dogs, that she seemed very nice and that the dogs were very well controlled. Sometimes on leads, sometimes loose, when presumably they answered to the whistle she wore round her neck, though as yet we'd never seen her use it. She'd certainly got them organised said Charles – it must save time in exercising them. Which apparently occurred to Miss Wellington because in next to no time she too was sailing past with a collection of dogs on leads.

They weren't hers. Miss Wellington had a large black cat who wouldn't have stood for that. But she was fond of all animals. It was Miss Wellington who, years before, convinced quite wrongly that he wasn't getting enough exercise, had insisted on bringing a neighbour's mastiff down to the Valley, where she'd let him off his lead – he looked so sad on it, she said; like a Roman prisoner in chains in the Forum – and he'd immediately chased Solomon through a cloche in the garden and Sol had to have twelve stitches in his leg.

After that she'd concentrated on Annabel. Fortunately not to the extent of wanting to take her out, but she was always coming down to feed her. She made a great point about toasting Annabel's bread and one day she explained to me why. She always took all the crusts off her bread, she said – one never knew where the baker had been. And while I was still trying to think of something to say to that one – that was why she toasted the crusts before bringing them down to Annabel, she confided. She wouldn't give the dear little soul bread that might have germs.

The result of that was that while Annabel accepted bread in its normal state, germs and all, from other people, she expected it toasted from Miss Wellington as according to the laws of the Medes and Persians. On the one occasion when Miss W. brought her half a loaf of sliced – which she hadn't bothered to toast, she said, because it was safely wrapped by machine – Annabel snorted petulantly and tossed the lot in the air and Miss Wellington, highly impressed, said it only went to show.

Now she brought the toast accompanied by four or five motley dogs – who, she explained, hanging wildly on to their leads, she was exercising for various people who lived on the new estate.

A laudable idea indeed, belonging as they did either to pensioners or to households with small children where, during the week, there was nobody to exercise them properly. The snag was, being Miss Wellington, it wasn't long before she was letting them off their leads, too, because she thought they looked like prisoners in chains.

So there they were, happy exponents of canine lib., milling round Annabel's gate one morning while Miss Wellington doled out the hygienic toast, when one of them spotted Seeley coming back from his morning's walk. Normally he came down through the trees and would have seen them before he emerged from cover. As luck would have it, however, he appeared this time on the track itself, marching round the corner like the principal actor on a stage.

All would have been well even then if he'd nipped back the way he'd come. But with memories of how (in his opinion) he'd recently routed Nero, he paused, arched his back, advanced threateningly down the lane – and when one of the dogs went after him, so did the entire pack.

It was a most momentous scene. Miss Wellington blew her whistle – of which the dogs, not being trained to it as were the dog woman's, took no notice at all. I, having been talking to Miss Wellington over our own gate, jumped it and ran, shouting wildly, after the dogs. Charles shot down from the orchard like Mercury in gumboots. And Annabel grabbed the carrier bag dropped by Miss Wellington and poured a shower of toast all over the ground.

We could just about have bet on the next move. Round the corner, as if on cue, came Father Adams with a spade. 'Whass up now then?' he interestedly enquired, leaning on it and surveying the scene. 'Startin' up thee own Hunt or somethin'? And whass thee done wi' the fox?'

That annoyed Miss Wellington for a start. It didn't help either when I – Seeley was safely up a tree by now but I was still shaken by his escape – said she ought to keep those dogs on leads or not bring them out at all.

Icily (I could see we wouldn't be speaking for a while) she clipped the leads on their collars. Icily, for the next few days, she marched them past in tight formation. Jolly good job, said Seeley, watching with Shebalu from the safety of one of the windows – but I was sorry about it. I was fond of old Miss Wellington.

Eventually, again copying the dog lady, she turned up leading the dogs and pushing a pedal-bike. A high-saddled affair with a basket, which she must have had for years. Inside the Forestry gate she let the dogs off the leads, mounted the bike and pedalled, with head held high, up the track. Looking, with the dogs running after her, just like a huntsman on wheels.

'She'll come round,' said Charles, seeing me look regretfully after her. 'And at least she can't be a nuisance in there, taking the dogs along the track.'

Which only shows how wrong one can be. She practically started a stampede.

Eight

I WAS IN ON that, too. I was out riding with some friends one morning, on horses from the local stables, and there we were, cantering lightheartedly along one of the Forestry tracks, when we spotted somebody pushing a bike away ahead of us.

I knew who it was at once. No one else ever takes a bicycle into the Forest. Not only would nobody want to, what with the stones and the ruts and the precipitous uphill paths, but only Miss Wellington would have unearthed a fact that we ourselves didn't know – that bridle paths are, by law, for horses, pedestrians and *cyclists*.

There she was, anyway. Miss Wellington, her bicycle and the dogs, throwing up the dust from the summer-baked track like a caravan crossing the Sahara. We slowed immediately. Even so we soon caught up with her, the long legs of the horses moving like camels across the ground.

'Hi, Miss Wellington,' I said as we passed. But Miss Wellington didn't reply.

I rode on regretfully, leaving her in our wake, sorry to think we still weren't speaking. At least... I *thought* were leaving her in our wake. Suddenly I realised that Miss Wellington had mounted her bike and was bumping furiously along at the side of us. Not because she'd had second thoughts and wanted to make it up, but because she was determined she wasn't going to be passed.

We were walking the horses now. One never canters past people or other animals. Even so we were still raising the dust and Miss Wellington was getting whiter every minute. She was also ringing her bicycle bell. Right on a level with the horses' tails, and the dogs started yapping and, highly disciplined though they were, the horses didn't like it. Ears back, heads tossing, they fidgetted and quickened their step, which in turn raised a lot more dust.

'Let me pass,' said Miss Wellington imperiously. 'D'you hear me? You're covering me in dust. Will you please let me pass?'

We couldn't. Nothing short of a police horse would have stood still for that cacophony to pass it. We began to trot. Miss Wellington, still ringing her bell, pedalled correspondingly faster. Like the opening of the Charge at Omdurman (except, of course, for the bike), we swept close-packed in the dust along the lane, emerged at last into a clearing – wheeled smartly to the right across the grass and were off and away up another track before Miss Wellington realised what we were doing.

The horses, freed from the bicycle bell and the yapping dogs, went up the track like thunderbolts. 'Silly old fool,' said one of the other riders. 'If these hadn't been bomb-proof horses...'

They weren't all that bomb-proof at that. Pepe, the one I was riding, always leapt at the beginning of a canter anyway and after Miss Wellington's frustrations he went into the air like Pegasus. Jasper, the big full-thoroughbred black, had only been held in check by the coolness and skill of his rider.

'Silly old fool,' echoed Charles when he heard about it. 'She'll come a cropper one of these days.'

She did. Though fortunately not off her bike. Somewhere up in the Forest one morning she let the dogs off their leads, one of them spotted a rabbit – a rare enough occurrence since myxomatosis, but the rabbits are definitely coming back – and though three of them returned to her from the chase that followed, the fourth one just simply vanished. Hours after I'd seen her go through the Forestry gate – so long, indeed, that I thought she'd done a circular tour and must have been home hours ago – she appeared, hat awry, in the lane outside, clutching the other three dogs and her bicycle.

Gone now was this business of not speaking. 'I've lost little Maybelle,' she informed me tearfully. 'I don't know what to do... she's terribly old... what will Mrs Warland say?'

Mrs Warland, I gathered, was the owner. And Maybelle – casting a quick eye over the remainder of the pack – must be the bad-tempered poodle with the sticking-out teeth who'd initiated the chase after Seeley. All the same, she was someone's dog and she might have got stuck in a rabbit-hole...

If she liked to take the other dogs home, I told Miss Wellington, Charles and I would go up and search. We didn't need to go far. Having called Charles down from the orchard, dumped the pastry I was making in the refrigerator and put on my boots, we were just going up the Forestry track when we spotted a dun-coloured figure puffing towards us. Teeth protruding, poodle-legs twinkling, Maybelle was on her way home. She didn't stop for us – not even at our gate, where lost dogs and horses tend to accumulate. Straight on up the hill she went and in through Miss Wellington's gate. Obviously Maybelle's stomach had felt the call of elevenses.

We hadn't done a thing, but Miss Wellington insisted we had. Whenever she brought the dogs past after that, Maybelle, securely on her rhinestoned lead, was instructed to Speak to the Nice Friends who'd Rescued Her. Maybelle, knowing that for a load of codswallop, lifted a dun-coloured lip at us and snarled. If the cats were in evidence Miss Wellington also, with fine disregard for personal safety, lifted Maybelle to shoulder height so that she could see them too and told her to Speak to the Dear Little Kitties. Maybelle did. At which Seeley had to be restrained and spent the next half-hour growling out of the window, Shebalu crossed her eyes and sat for safety on a doortop – and how Miss Wellington got Maybelle to the ground without, in the process, losing her nose was a continual testimonial to what Father Adams was always saying: 'The Lord looks after Fools'.

We were back on speaking terms with her, anyway, which was one good thing. And before long she gave up the dog-exercising business. It was too much of a responsibility, she said. And she always had the dogs in her kitchen after their walk and in winter they'd make everything so dirty... So, after crisis, we returned to normal. Only the original dog-lady exercised dogs en masse and hers were as well-ordered as Diana's; Miss Wellington, once more on foot, returned to good works in the village; and the cats – we could hardly believe it – went on being as good as gold.

It was all so different from when Seeley had been a kitten. Then, having no one to play with, he was always going off on his own. There was the time, for instance, when he'd scared us over the fox-holes. We'd taken him with us when we went up to examine some trees, high up in our woods, which kept the sun off the cottage in the evening. Huge sycamores – which, said Charles, not only blocked out the sun but were a positive menace to his fruit trees. Digging near some apple tree roots, a good twenty yards away, he'd found sycamore roots intermingled with them, attracted there by all the watering he did and the food in the soil from the fertilisers. It was marvellous, admittedly, to think of roots being able to track down food and water... travelling through the soil like moles, a good twenty yards to reach their goal... but they were taking the nourishment from the apple trees; the sycamores would have to come down.

So there we were, debating the best way to do it so they wouldn't crash on the apple trees anyway, and there was Seeley, still a tubby little kitten, exploring in all directions as we talked, and suddenly – when he thought we were suitably distracted – he was away across our boundary path and into the neighbouring woods. Uncultivated these were – a tangle of saplings and thorn bushes and low-growing brambles into which Seeley promptly vanished as into a jungle.

I plunged to my hands and knees immediately and scrambled after him, terrified of letting such a little mite go off on his own in fox country – and when, with threads pulled on my sweater and scratches everywhere, I eventually caught sight of him again, all my fears about foxes were crystallised. Seeley – small, so vulnerable-looking and never more dear to me than in that moment of peril, was standing in the entrance to a fox-earth. A huge, dark, gaping hole in the hillside which, from the freshness of the soil around it, was certainly inhabited and quite possibly recently dug. Even as I spotted him he vanished inside the hole... and even as I shouted for Charles he popped back out again. Not to come to me, however. That section of the woods was positively cratered with fox-earths. Seeley pranced across in front of me, almost within arm's reach – and then nipped tantalisingly down another.

My fear, knowing his inquisitiveness, was that he might go on down one of those passages. Down there somewhere was a fox. Maybe a vixen with cubs. Seeley wouldn't have a chance if he met up with her. So, afraid to go nearer in case it made him go deeper in, I kept calling him imploringly – and every few seconds he flashed out of a hole, yelled at me that Here he Was, this game was Fun, wasn't it? – and then went down another.

We avoided Nemesis on that occasion by Charles crawling through the thicket on his hands and knees as well, crouching behind the fox-hole down which the truant was at the moment – and then, as I called 'Seeley-weeley-weeley' from a distance and he emerged once more to tantalise me, grabbing him like lightning before he realised Charles was there.

We couldn't take him back through the brambles. With him hanging protesting down my back – I held on to his legs while Charles, as best he could, made a way for me to push through – we got him over the top fence, into a field, through the field gate and back down the lane.

We'd Tricked Him, howled Seeley, broadcasting his wrath to the Valley as we went. He was going Right Back In There, he bawled, struggling like mad as we passed the spot where he'd first gone in. He'd go back again as soon as he Could, anyway, he promised me, as, holding him in a grip of iron, I carted him, still struggling, back to the cottage.

Which was why I was so pleased when the next morning, instead of making straight for the wood with the fox-earths when we let him out, he ambled innocently off up the Forestry lane. After breakfast, to be on the safe side, I went out and called him. He appeared as if by magic, though I couldn't tell from which direction. It did strike me as odd that his legs were dry while the undergrowth was sopping wet, but it was only a passing thought. If one analysed everything with Siamese cats, sooner or later one would go bonkers. The main thing was that he was approximately where we'd left him. For once he hadn't wandered off...

That was what I thought. On my way back from posting some letters that afternoon the owner of the most striking house in the district – Spanish-cubist style and right at the top of the village – asked me if he'd come home all right. He'd been up to see her that morning, she said. She'd found him sitting in the patio entrance just as if he belonged there; she could hardly believe it when she opened the door and saw him. When she held her hand out, however, he got up and walked away. Down the road through the village, which explained why his legs had stayed dry.

She couldn't think why he'd favoured her, she said. I could. Her house was a lot more imposing than ours and Seeley obviously fancied looking as though he lived there, just as Solomon, years before, had liked the new house up the lane. What was more the next morning, in spite of all precautions, Seeley vanished again. This, said Charles, when we'd crawled without avail up to the fox-earths and peered frustratedly over the wall round the Spanish patio, was getting beyond a joke. Which house, for goodness' sake, was that blasted cat fancying himself in now?

Sam's and Dinah's down the lane, as a matter of fact. When I caught up with him he was sitting on *their* patio, trying it out for the effect.

After a record like that it was like a miracle to find him always in the garden with Shebalu. Even Annabel was intrigued. She spent ages watching them from her field up behind the cottage, mouth pouted, ears pointed straight towards them, looking, with her big white door-knocker nose, as solemn as an owl.

One day I was the intrigued one, however. Seeley and Shebalu were in the wide garden border under the hillside – Seeley looking at something under a delphinium, Shebalu importantly watching crouched by his side. Behind the border rose a high stone wall over which Annabel normally couldn't see – the retaining wall which holds back the hillside out of which the garden is carved. She was looking over it now, however. Reared up, with her head above the top of it, as tall as a sixteen-hand hunter. She was, I discovered after my initial reaction that I must be seeing things, standing with her front legs deliberately on an anthill.

That, said Charles, was really clever. Who said donkeys didn't have brains? Self-taught, too, I echoed. One thing was certain. We could always get her a job in a circus.

Nine

THINGS SEEMED TO BE going pretty smoothly just then. We had our minor alarms, of course. Sometimes in duplicate, as on the occasion when Charles came in to say that something had dug a huge hole in front of the paeony, it looked like a fox to him... adding, by way of encore, that Seeley was sitting on Shebalu in the conservatory and did I think that was all right?

That was easily dealt with. The hole, I said, had been dug by me the previous night, in the dark. Getting earth for earthboxes because I couldn't find the peat. And Seeley sitting on Shebalu meant it was time for her operation. All the more so, I said, when Charles said she seemed to be enjoying it. We'd better ring the Vet without delay.

There was another alarm the night we heard Seeley nattering when we were in bed – followed, after a pause, by a mysterious rattling noise. Charles, on the alert for intruders, was up in an instant, walking stick at the ready. I wasn't. My interpretation was that Seeley was talking to himself as Solomon used to do and that Shebalu, having been disturbed by him, was pushing her food-dish around, probably to show her annoyance. He'd better go down and check, said Charles. If he did they'd be upstairs and under the bed, I warned him. Walking over us all night and we wouldn't get any sleep...

Having thus deterred him it was my fault entirely that we lay awake for hours anyway, convincing ourselves that it *was* a plate being pushed around and not somebody breaking in, and that it wasn't till the morning that we discovered the cause of the trouble. The cats slept on a rug on the settee, with a hotwater bottle under it and another rug round them to keep out the draught. I fixed their bed, Charles filled the hotwater bottle and dumped it on the settee, and I put it in place under the rug. Usually, that is. The previous night I'd overlooked it. All night long the bottle had lain exposed on top of their bed. Too hot to sit on, taking up space that they ought to be in... hence Seeley's worried nattering and Shebalu's clattering her plate around.

The length of a twenty-foot room she'd pushed it, till she got it against the door into the hall. The nearest she could get to us and that was where she'd been rattling it. Either to attract our attention or to make sure that if she wasn't going to get any sleep, she'd see to it that we jolly well didn't either.

Looking at her, so small and white and feminine, it was difficult to imagine her capable of such deliberate thinking. She roused in everybody, including Seeley, a desire to protect her from the dangers of the wicked world and conveyed an impression of such ethereal frailty one felt that one cross word and she'd be off to join the angels. In fact she outclassed Seeley by miles when it came to thinking. Charles said it resulted from her being city-bred; Seeley, he said, was more of the country gentleman.

As for frailty... no kitten could have taken more knocks than she did and come up bouncing. She had a habit of rushing out of ambush and trying to gallop alongside our feet and she was tripped over, trodden on – kicked even, on occasion. Didn't Matter, she would assure us, picking herself up from the latest collision and tearing headlong on her way. And within seconds, sure as Fate, she'd be in collision again.

Sometimes we wondered whether that was why she was so crossed-eyed. Concussed when she was young, said Charles, in a suitably sombre voice. It wasn't that initially, of course. Turned-in eyes are hereditary with many Siamese. But she did squint more pronouncedly after she'd had a bang. At times we got really worried.

Gradually, however, we noticed that it coincided with moments of stress. She squinted when she was annoyed, she did it when she was concentrating, she did it when she was willing us to get her ball with a bell out of the bureau... Seeley always regarded us with the straightest gaze in the world, but when Shebalu was thinking she looked like Ben Turpin.

Cross-eyed or not, we already loved her dearly, and when the day arrived for her to be spayed gloom hung like a pall over the household. Over Shebalu because she couldn't have any breakfast, over Seeley because she wasn't allowed out into the garden with him, and over us because we knew what lay ahead of her. It had to be done, of course. We didn't want her as a breeding cat – we wanted her as Seeley's friend. And once Siamese come on heat they can become so hysterical that it's a case of either letting them breed, going berserk or having them spayed. Safe though it is, however, there is always risk in an operation and Siamese, particularly, can be tricky with anaesthetics. Years before we'd lost our first cat, Sugieh, when she was spayed.

The depression hung over the cottage all the morning. 'Ring at three,' the Vet had said when we left her at his surgery. 'She may be round by then and we can tell you when you can fetch her.' At one we had lunch. Coffee and biscuits and cheese. Neither of us had appetite for any more. At two, sitting waiting, we checked on our watches. They appeared to be still going. Charles checked his again to make sure. At three, on the dot – 'You ring,' I said to Charles. My legs were shaking too much for me to walk to the phone.

She was all right. Still very dopey, of course, said the Vet. We could fetch her at six o'clock.

'Gosh, I feel hungry,' I said when I heard the news. Charles said he was starving.

It was a far different drive to the Vet's this time. Swishing through the lanes of burnished copper... it was autumn now and the leaves were coming down. Enjoying the picture of the sun setting low across the fields, and the smoke rising lazily from cottage chimneys. There was such a peaceful, secure feeling about it all – and in us, too, now that we knew our girl was safe.

She even, when we saw her, looked better than we expected. Sitting in her basket eyeing us with a placid almond stare. She'd done very well, said Mr Horler. All the same he recommended that we left her in her basket for the night. It would be best not to let her out, however much she asked. Not that she was likely to want to; she'd be still very weak on her legs.

So we drove her gently home, put her basket in front of the fire, admitted Seeley from the hall in the role of invalid's visitor – and instead of sniffing at her warily as we expected him to do, on account of the smell of the anaesthetic, he stuck a large black paw straight in through the bars and gave her a couple of hearty prods. Even as we jumped to pull him away, too, a blue paw came sparring out in return, reaching out full length to try to prod him back. Come on Out then, mrr-mrred Seeley, rolling enticingly on his back. She would if she Could, waaaahed his small blue friend, starting to roll on hers.

We did think of ringing Horler. Knowing us and the crises we could produce, he was probably sitting at home expecting it. But if we did and he still instructed us to keep her confined, without doubt she would burst her stitches.

'Let her out,' decided Charles. 'If we've got to call him later, then we shall have to.' So we unlatched the wire door of the basket, out she tottered – and that apparently was all she wanted. For the rest of the evening she lay regally before the fire like the queen after whom she was named.

We talked to her. Seeley washed her. He couldn't think where she'd *been*, he mrr-mrred worriedly; it was going to take days to make her smell right. The fire played on her and she squinted contentedly when we looked at her. It was nice to be home she said.

That was all right until bedtime. Then, having decided it would be better for her to sleep on her own – officially, after all, she was still supposed to be in her basket – we made her a bed on the hearthrug, put water and an earthbox within reach, picked up Seeley who could hardly believe his luck, and started towards the door. Shebalu without more ado, got up and staggered after us. She made no sound. Just, with a dogged determination that wrung our hearts, set out on the long, painful trek the length of the room. We'd done this before – the first night she Came, she reproached Charles when he rushed to pick her up. Why were we leaving her behind? Didn't we like her? What had she done that we were going to leave her down there on her own?

We couldn't take her with us in her condition. We dare not risk her jumping off the bed. So, there being nothing else we could do, we left Seeley with her to comfort her. We came down twice in the night to make sure his idea of being a comfort wasn't wrestling with her or practising kicking her in the stomach, all of which Charles imagined going on in the silence below. On each occasion they were lying before the fire together – her back against his stomach, her head against his shoulder, two faces raised to us like a pair of furry angels. Seeley squeezed his eyes when he saw us looking in at them. He was taking care of her, he said. She'd be all right in the morning.

She was too. By breakfast-time she was up and about and eating like a horse. And then, just when we thought we could relax for awhile, we discovered a leak in the roof.

It was the fault of the starlings who'd taken over, years before, from the jackdaws who'd lived in our spare room chimney. It wasn't a working chimney. The fireplace beneath it had been blocked in long ago. And we'd felt rather honoured to play host to a pair of jackdaws. They raised several families in the chimney-pot and obviously regarded us as friends.

When, one Spring, we found starlings there in their place, I felt it was rather a come-down. We'd had starlings around when I'd lived in town as a child, but the jackdaws had been so unusual. Ours had been the only pair in the Valley. Where they'd gone we never knew. Probably found a chimney considered more imposing, said Charles. Like Seeley's fancying other people's porches.

Whatever the reason there, in their place, was a possessive pair of starlings – evolving in due course into a very thriving colony as the children, growing up, stayed on the parental estate; merely overflowing into our roof.

It was like one of those village paintings by Brueghel, only with birds instead of people. Birds coming out of the chimneypot (the original pair presumably, still living in starling headquarters); birds coming out from the sides of the roof; and some through the front, into the guttering. These last emerged through very small holes through which they squeezed flat on their stomachs. The struggling and scrambling of feet as they went in and out was really quite alarming and at nesting time, when they were carrying in materials, it must have been pretty exhausting. More than one bird dropped its quota of sticks and bits trying to manoeuvre them in through the hole and there was always somebody eyeing us ruffle-feathered from the guttering, having just squeezed out and, from the look on his face, disgusted with us for not providing a bigger opening.

From the noise of hammering which went on inside the roof as some ambitious tenant improved on his quarters I wondered why they didn't enlarge the entrance holes themselves while they were at it. That, said Charles, showed their intelligence. They knew we had cats around and they'd deliberately left small entrances. They didn't want any Siamese cats getting in at them through the gutters.

They needn't have worried at that time. Sheba was with us then, and though in her young days the climb would have been nothing to her – many a time she'd gone up the roof at the back and appeared, tail raised, rubbing round a chimney pot – now she was old and far past climbing. As for Seeley, with his head for heights, he'd as soon have thought of climbing the Empire State Building. He sometimes looked up at the guttering as he passed beneath it – at which time there was invariably somebody above to peer beadily down at him and scold him. On one occasion, too (was it, we wondered, deliberate?), one dropped some sticks down on him instead of taking them in for nest construction. Seeley pretended he hadn't noticed. Must have started to rain, he said.

Charles said he liked the starlings. Did I realise, he enquired, that they were one of the most intelligent birds in existence? One of the few birds with two lobes to their brains, which is something they share with human beings? Among the few small birds, as a result, who walk instead of hop? We had a marvellous opportunity, if only we took it, to study them at close quarters.

We certainly did. They used to wake me up in the morning demonstrating their walking prowess over our bedroom ceiling. One of them must have had long-distance ambitions; he pattered backwards and forwards for hours. The one who'd gone in for a home extension – he kept pretty busy, too. Tapping eternally away at his project – it was just like a man with a hammer.

Probably pecking out some of the old lathe and plaster to make a nesting hole, said Charles – there must be lots of it still up inside the roof. He couldn't think why I was worried. Of *course* they wouldn't make the roof collapse.

They did the next best thing. Given carte blanche on account of they'd chosen to live with a bird-watcher... making any structural alterations that suited their taste... they eventually made an entrance at the bottom of the chimney pot, which we didn't know about until it rained.

Ten

IT WAS QUITE SIMPLE. Just a matter of their raising a couple of tiles to make a way in. In the normal way we'd probably have noticed the damp patch on the ceiling, righted the displaced tiles and that would have been that. Only it happened that it didn't rain normally. It came down in an absolute deluge and we woke up in the morning to find that the stream was overflowing. Swirling down the lane in a fast-running torrent that threatened to wash all the surface off the track.

We were so busy seeing to that... knee-deep in icy water, rodding the pipes under the drive and hooking debris out of the ditches to get the stream back into its proper course, that it was some hours before – still breakfastless – I went upstairs to change out of my wet clothes, heard a splashing sound in the spare room and found that the rain was coming in.

It was dripping as hard as it could go, through the ceiling rose, down the electric light flex and on to the seat of a chair and Charles wasn't at all pleased at having to go up on the roof, also still breakfastless, and put the tiles to rights. All the more so as, while he was sitting astride the apex, one arm round the chimney pot hoping it wouldn't come off. Miss Wellington came past and called up 'Having trouble with the roof?' 'No,' I heard Charles reply. 'I'm just admiring the view.'

Which, as I told him afterwards, was a silly thing to say because Miss Wellington would believe he meant it, sure as eggs were eggs, and pass it on to the rest of the village.

All was well that ended well, though, as I remarked, rather tiredly, later. We'd just had a meal and I'd lit a fire and put an oil-heater in the hall to dry things out a bit. Charles had said we'd better keep the electricity off for a while in case it shorted on account of the wire getting damp. So there we sat, Charles in his usual armchair, I on the hearthrug with my back against the settee. Seeley was on my lap, Shebalu against my legs, all of us relaxing, for a few blissful minutes...

We fell asleep of course. What with our exertions in the stream and on the roof and now the soothing warmth of the fire. A while later I opened one eye and thought 'Gosh – the fire's smoking. How odd. It doesn't seem very windy.' It would die down presently, I decided, and closed my eyes again. There was nothing I could do about it. I was too tired, anyway.

Still later I opened my eyes once more. By now the room was really foggy. I could hardly see the Welsh dresser across it while Shebalu, usually so outstandingly white, looked positively grey against my legs. She had her head raised too, and was puzzledly sniffing. The fire must have been smoking, while we slept, like an oil-tanker. 'Oil-tanker!' I thought, starting up in alarm. I'd realised at last what it was.

I hadn't checked on the stove in the hall after lighting it, and it had been flaring up for nearly two hours. The hall and the staircase were blacked out solidly, with cobwebs hanging down like curtains, while the sitting room lay under a blanket of smuts – and so, when we went upstairs, did the bedrooms. Shebalu was grey for days, however much we brushed her. It was a good thing it didn't show on him, wasn't it? said Seeley, interestedly watching.

It showed everywhere else. Carpets, curtains, bedspreads, walls – I looked like a Kentucky minstrel. I got things clean eventually, of course – but as usual, I never learn. This happened within a week of Shebalu's spaying and one morning a friend rang up, while I was cooking breakfast, to ask how she was getting on. 'Fine,' I said enthusiastically. And then we discussed the heavy rain-storm and I told her the story of the black-out and we both of us laughed like drains. She said she'd had an oil-stove black-out once herself and we laughed a lot more at her experiences. 'Well, thank goodness everything's all right *now*,' I said, ringing off to go and finish getting the breakfast.

As I say, I never learn. I remember once, after Solomon had been ill, someone ringing up to ask how he was doing. 'Oh, he's fine now,' I'd replied, just as enthusiastically – and, putting down the phone, had come through the living room door just in time to see Sol raise his tail to me in greeting against the electric fire. Fortunately it had a guard over it, but within five seconds of saying he was fine, there we were with a horrible smell of singeing and Solomon's tail in tiger-stripes that didn't grow out for months.

Just as now, when I came through the same door to another smell of burning and, going out to the kitchen, found I hadn't turned off the cooker when the phone rang. I'd left two eggs in the grill pan with the grill going full blast, they were now burnt black and I couldn't see across the kitchen. The only room that had escaped, incidentally, when the oil-stove flared up the previous week.

I turned off the cooker, opened the back door to let out the smoke – through which Charles promptly appeared, like an agitated genie, announcing that Shebalu had taken out her stitches. Not all of them, I discovered, rushing to see for myself. Of her original three she'd taken out one on either side but was still held together by the middle one. She stood on the kitchen table, vastly pleased with herself, while we inspected her and decided that, as there were only two days to go before she was due to have her stitches removed anyway, if we made sure she didn't get excited and run up trees, possibly, with a bit of luck, she might hold out.

We lectured her about this, released her – and, the kitchen door being open to let out the smoke, out shot Shebalu and up on to the hillside where, her legs feeling free, no doubt, after the constricting pull of the stitches, she promptly went up a pine tree. Later that day, too, she fell off the piano. Luck was with us, however. The remaining stitch stayed put.

So that was another hurdle over and now we could settle down to a period of quiet domesticity, with the holidays over, Shebalu safely spayed, little to be done in the garden and the prospect of cosy winter evenings round the fire with neighbours and friends. We never seemed to have time for entertaining in the summer and it was nice, now, to be asking people in again.

Or was it, with two Siamese cats and Charles in on the preparations? I remember one day, when we had people coming, getting out the vacuum to give the place the once-over and discovering that one of the pins was missing from the plug. That, I realised, must have been the long thin brass thing I'd found on the landing the previous morning. But where on earth had I put it? On the bedroom shelf? I could actually see myself doing it – but when I looked, it wasn't there. Of course, now I remembered – it was on the spare room tallboy... except that when I went to get it, it wasn't there either. Or on the Welsh dresser in the sitting room, or on the chest in the hall. So, with an hour to go, I started crawling round the floor with the hand-vacuum. Accompanied by two extremely curious cats with their noses to the ground like bloodhounds.

What was I looking for? That mouse he'd lost? asked Seeley. Interesting, wasn't it? said Shebalu, completely engrossed. Surely I remembered what I'd done with it, said Charles. Not the way things were in this house, I said. It was a wonder I knew where I was myself at times.

At last I'd finished tidying the sitting room, however, and the food was prepared and spread round on cupboard-tops and in the refrigerator... no good taking chances with two Sherlock Holmes around. I must remember to put them out in the hall at supper-time, too, I thought. We didn't want a repeat of the last time people dropped in.

On that occasion, with Seeley voluntarily in the hall, watching in the moonlight for things moving out in the lane, we'd let Shebalu stay in with us while we had coffee and a snack. Impressed, obviously, by the honour thus conferred on her she sat gravely before the fire, paws tucked under, with the air of being a Big Cat now, thinking on serious things. Until that was, we'd put the table over the top of her. 'Please don't disturb her,' our visitors had pleaded. 'Dear little soul... we don't mind her being there.'

Within minutes the dear little soul was discovered stealing the butter. Standing on her hind legs with a blob of it on her nose. 'Oh – don't do that,' our friends protested gallantly as I took the butter dish away to change it – but who fancies butter all grooved with kittens' teeth?

So I had that in mind... and I cleaned the bathroom... bath immaculate, polished floor, clean towels on the rails... which produced Charles as automatically as if I'd put a coin in a slot-machine, announcing that he'd finished in the orchard and now he'd have his bath.

Oh no he wasn't, I said – not with the Allinsons due in half an hour. So he obligingly washed instead and all I had to do was re-clean the washbasin, re-change the towels, pick up the lumps of mud which had fallen out of his turn-ups and repolish the floor and all was well. Except that just as I was putting the fresh towels on the rails the cats rushed in in a 'We've got visitors coming' steeple-chase, Seeley went straight up me and I dropped the towels down the lavatory.

Next, I thought, getting out a fresh lot of towels and refusing to be deterred, for oil in the stove in the hall. It was working properly now and the night was rather cold. I'd better go up to the garage for the oil myself, though. Charles was changing by this time and I didn't want to put him off.

So up I went. It is rarely I visit the garage; Charles's idea of storing things reduces me to despair. This time I came back more despairing than ever, though I had managed to find the oil.

'Is all that stuff up there supposed to be a burglar trap?' I enquired. 'What stuff?' asked Charles, whose own mental picture of the garage is a cross between an operating theatre and the engine room of the Queen Elizabeth.

'That brick right in the middle of the side doorway,' I said. 'So that when you go in you turn your foot on it and nearly break your ankle.'

That, said Charles with dignity, was for use as a door-stop when the door was open.

'All those pieces of wood propped up behind the brick, that you have to climb over like a barricade before you can get inside the place?'

Those, said Charles, were lengths he was going to use for Annabel's new stable. Brought out of store ready, so they were to hand when he wanted them.

'That old broomhead without any bristles, right where when you've mountaineered over the wood you step down straight on to it?'

That, said Charles, very righteously, was there to be brought down for *burning*. He was starting to clean out the garage. I was always complaining about the muddles.

Quite speechless, I filled the stove, took off the covers we normally have on the chair arms to protect them from Siamese claws, set the tea trolley... not with any food, of course; that was still on top of the cupboards; just with the china and the cutlery and the cut-glass jug for the cream. At which point (I could have bet on it) the cats appeared again.

Look what She'd found, said Shebalu. Some nice yellow chair arms that hadn't been clawed yet. Look what He'd found, came a familiar voice from the passage outside the kitchen. All those books had been moved off the tea-trolley and you could play circus cats through the shelves...

So, of course, we had another steeplechase. Over the chair arms, through the trolley – straight through the china, too, but fortunately none of it was broken. Gathering them up into one large, blue and seal bundle I shut them out into the hall. Almost immediately Charles went upstairs and let them in again.

Now *look*, I said, fielding Shebalu, carrying her once more out to the hall and depositing her on the chest. I was *busy*. Couldn't she behave herself? Did she *want* to end up in a home for bad cats?

Who? Her? asked Shebalu, rubbing coyly against a jug of flowers. It was Seeley who'd knocked over those cups. She was a Good Girl, she was, she added, rubbing against the jug again for luck.

It was unfortunate that she'd chosen to demonstrate her innocence against my flower arrangement. Absolute ages it had taken me, being hopeless at that sort of thing. Some sprays of those beech leaves from the bazaar and a few huge, exotic paper poppies... one or two copper-sprayed teazles and some dried achillea to fill it out... It looked quite good now, even though I said it myself... until Shebalu, busily pursuing her demonstration of being a good girl, went right round the jug in a circle; tail raised, pushing lovingly against the leaves... and the whole arrangement, being lightweight, sailed round with her and ended up back to front.

Even that wasn't the end of it. Hastily re-shuffling the flowers – though obviously they'd never look the same again – we were ready on time, our friends arrived, the cats were shut out in the hall while we ate, according to plan...

I did think I heard a bang a while later, but it was followed by the scampering of feet so obviously all was well. Probably Shebalu had fallen off the piano again, I thought. Or Seeley was practising jumping off the bed.

What it actually was was Shebalu putting paid to my flower display for good and all. After supper one of our friends, going out to get her handbag, came back to say that something was lying flat on the floor in the hall. A few bits of leaves, when I looked, and an overturned container. The rest had fallen – or had it been pushed? – behind the chest.

How on earth had that happened? said Shebalu, advancing innocently down the stairs as we stood there looking at it. That was the trouble – those artificial things were always so light. Then, with Seeley behind her, she made her entrance into the sitting room. Everybody waiting to see them? they said.

Eleven

WE WOULDN'T HAVE HAD things otherwise, all the same. Seeley's insistence on having his breakfast in the conservatory even though summer was over... Shebalu's perambulations with the dish-mop, the pot-scourer and now – her latest addiction – empty egg-shells which she stole before I could put them in the dustbin, prowled round with them in her mouth for ages being a Sinister White Jungle cat with her prey and then, when she decided she wasn't impressing us any longer, poked primly under an armchair to demonstrate how feminine and tidy she was... these expressions of individuality were why we had Siamese cats.

True we had our moments when we wished they weren't quite so individual. When, for instance, holding a plate aloft like a wine-waiter, announcing 'Breakfast for Seeley' loudly as I went because that was part of the formula and he wouldn't go without it, preceded by a large Siamese cat who also bawled about it being his Breakfast every inch of the way – when that little procession rounded the corner on its way to the conservatory, and it was blowing half a gale or raining and someone happened to be sitting in a car in the lane... at times like that I did feel rather embarrassed. As I did these days when visitors pushed back their armchairs and under them, however much I'd searched, there was always the odd abandoned half of an eggshell.

But then there were the times when they showed their affection for us. Shebalu perched on Charles's shoulder while he read, for instance, pretending she was reading herself, her eyes deep-crossed in utter bliss. Or Seeley seeking me out for one of his bouts of snogging, which was one of his individualities. For this he jumped on a table or chair-back – anything that gave him height – reared himself up at me and put his paws on my shoulders. Then, eyes closed, he'd rub his head against my face – a big long swoosh across one cheek and then across the other. He'd keep it up, on alternate cheeks, for minutes at a time. General de Seal, Charles dubbed him, watching him do it – and in fact it was exactly like someone giving an accolade.

They were so fond of each other, too. Talking to one another, calling if one was missing, lying before the fire together, their outstretched paws intertwined. Though Seeley sometimes now slept underneath his rug indoors – a thing he used to do only in his cage. Was he expecting a cold winter? we wondered. Or did he hope that way to get some peace from Shebalu who, if she wasn't asleep herself, would never let him alone?

He pretended to get annoyed when she tormented him – flattening his ears and jumping on her and biting her furiously back. Didn't know what children were Coming To, he'd wail at her aggrievedly. He'd leave home if she wasn't careful. He'd go up to the pub, only he didn't drink.

That was when we were around. When he thought we weren't, he'd be under the rug but with his tail sweeping seductively across the hearth like a pendulum, and Shebalu prancing and pouncing on it with delight. Nobody talking about leaving home now. Only, when Shebalu looked like stopping, a large black paw coming out and slyly poking her to egg her on again.

So we moved on towards the winter – and if one aspect of its approach which puzzled passers-by was my marching solemnly through wind and weather conducting Seeley to his breakfast in the conservatory, another, which mystified them even more, was Charles transferring his fish.

When he'd built the pond in the yard he'd constructed it with a deep centre edged with stones and a shallow rim around that which was only some six inches deep. Normally the pond was filled to the brim and the fish could enjoy themselves all over it. They did, too – basking under the water lily leaves, gliding gracefully out over the stones, racing each other in excited shoals the length of the long outer rim. When and if they spawned, however, which we encouraged by putting water-weed in the shallow part – the idea then was that one lowered the level of the water, confined the large fish to the centre, and left the eggs, and later the fry, out in the rim beyond the stones, safe from the risk of being eaten. That was the theory. In practice, as fish spawn principally after spring and summer rain, which puts oxygen into the water and generally brisks things up, we never could keep the level down. The rain always raised it again, the fish got out over the stones... wriggling sideways over them or on their stomachs and that didn't do their skins any good... and either they had a cannibal feast or, if we got there first, we rescued the eggs with a teaspoon and hatched them out in jars.

All that happened in the shallow part, in fact, was that they ran races in it, spawned in it – and, in the winter, got frozen in it. However much we baled it out, trying to keep them in the deep part for the winter, it always rained, re-filled the rim, the fish got out into it – and a night or two later it froze and the fish were trapped in the ice. We rescued them, revived them in tepid water, returned them to their wiser relatives in the centre – but so often the slimy protective covering of their bodies had been damaged by the ice or stones, and when the weather warmed up the fish got fungus on the damaged parts and died.

Charles was attached to his fish and, having reared them from inch-long tiddlers to fine, fat, king-sized carp, was determined not to lose any more of them this winter. He was going to bring them indoors, he announced. Where? I enquired, having visions of their spending the winter in the bath. In the conservatory, said Charles. In what? I asked. He'd think of something, he said. And, sure enough, he did.

If passers-by (and, as there is only a low wall round the cottage garden, our activities are as open to the public gaze as the stage in Shakespeare's time)... if passers-by were intrigued by the sight of a fishing-net hanging from our coalhouse roof for weeks (those fish were as wily as trout, said Charles; the only way to catch them was to take them by surprise)... if they stood open-mouthed at the sight of Charles, when he'd caught one, running, net before him, up the garden... if all that shook them, they'd have been rocked to their foundations if they'd seen the set-up in the conservatory. Where, being another of Charles's inspirations, the fish were swimming around in a cider cask.

He'd bought four of them the previous spring – huge things, iron-banded, nearly six feet high, and reeking to high heaven of the local cider. Sawn in half – which they'd obligingly done at the cider farm – these were Charles's idea of tubs in which to grow his blueberries. Our soil is lime, and blueberries must be in peat, and the whole thing was perfectly logical. Except that, as usual, people didn't know this and the appearance of eight huge half cider casks at our gate aroused considerable speculation.

'Whass they for, then?' asked Father Adams. Even he was at a loss for words when I told him. Ern Biggs decided their use for himself. He told people they were for my home-made wine. What with horses jibbing at passing them, people coming down to have a look at them, Ern Biggs's tale given credence by the fact that the garden now had a distinct aura of alcohol – I could have sunk through the ground over those casks. Even when Charles with considerable difficulty, had rolled seven of them up into the orchard, people still came by and speculated. 'D'ee reckon they be really makin' wine in they?' I heard one say. 'Maybe they'm for treadin' the grapes,' came the thoughtful reply.

Eventually it became obvious that Charles was growing something in them. People still wanted to know what, of course, and looked curiously up as they passed. 'Wortleberries from up on the hill,' advised Ern, who knew nothing of cultivated blueberries. So they shook their heads and classed us as bonkers anyway. Who'd grow little old 'urts in bloomin' great cider tubs? And of course there was still the eighth and unused half-tub, parked emptily at the side of the drive...

Through the summer and autumn it stayed there, waiting for Charles to move it. And when finally he did and it could be seen through the conservatory window, Ern's excitement knew no bounds. 'Started thee wine then. Whass be making? Parsnip?' he enquired, craning his neck from the gate. I avoided telling him that we were keeping fish in it. Heaven knows what he'd have made of that. But there they were. And was it my imagination, or did they zig-zag more than usual as they swam?

They were protected from the weather, at any rate. And Seeley didn't bother about them when he was in there having his breakfast, while Shebalu wasn't interested in the conservatory during the winter. She stayed indoors, except for her morning outings. Driving us crazy with her ball with the bell on which, when she wasn't towing the dish-mop or stowing eggshells under chairs, she carried about perpetually, like a child with a favourite rag doll.

This wasn't her original ball. That at least had been big enough to see. This was another old one of Seeley's, which before that had belonged to Solomon, and she'd found it for herself in some forgotten corner. Such a small, bedraggled object you couldn't even tell when she had it in her mouth. All you could hear was the tinkling of the bell.

What it had beyond any of her other toys we couldn't imagine. That she had found it for herself, perhaps; that it was small and it appealed to her to carry it; or perhaps it had an air about it of having been loved by other cats. At any rate it was now Shebalu's favourite toy. She toted it around during the day, expected us to throw it for her at night... she would have made a jolly good gun dog, said Charles. She never got tired of retrieving.

Maybe so. Except that gun dogs, in my experience, don't park their trophies under the furniture. And then sit down and howl because they can't remember where they put them.

Shebalu was forever doing that. Not when she tired of playing with it, because she never did. But when I got tired of throwing it she'd carry it round in her mouth for a while and then, as she did with the eggshells, tuck it carefully under a chair or somewhere while she spoke to Seeley or had a drink. Minutes later, when she wanted it again, the bawling would start. Either she'd pushed it too far under something and now she couldn't reach it or else – and this caused havoc – she'd forgotten where it was.

Wanted her Ball! she'd wail, getting on her stomach and peering hopefully under the settee. Very antique it was. She didn't want to lose it. Had he seen her Ball? she'd demand of Charles, reaching up to tap his knee and fixing him with worried blue eyes. By the time she'd done a bit more shouting she'd have us all looking for her ball. Even Seeley was going round with me peering intently under the chairs. When we found it, too, she gathered it up like a long-lost child – first giving it a little snort to show it how cross she was – and then, if I still wouldn't throw it for her, promptly poking it under something again.

Once it was missing for days, and so despondent she looked, sitting waiting for it in the middle of the carpet, that I practically spring-cleaned the cottage, thinking of places it might be and not being able to rest until I'd gone and searched them.

I thought it was gone for good that time. A few days previously she'd been playing with it while I was cleaning the bathroom and she'd put it down the lavatory. Stood on her hind legs with the ball in her mouth, looked down for a moment and deliberately dropped it in. I'd fished it out and washed it, knowing how precious it was. Now I could only think she'd done it again and somebody had pulled the flush.

We had visitors when she found it. Shebalu was after the sandwiches and Charles put her out in the hall. That was odd, he said, coming back. He'd put her in the armchair and she'd actually stayed there instead of trying to race him in. She seemed to be interested in something behind the cushion. He supposed she hadn't put a mouse behind it?

Shebalu in fact had never seen a mouse as yet – but the look on our visitors' faces when Charles suggested there might be a dead one in the chair (they themselves had no experience of Siamese cats) was only equalled by their expression when a second later there came the tinkling of a bell and I, rushing to open the door, said 'She's found it! Thank heaven for that!'

She had too. In just about the one place I hadn't looked because I'd never known her put it there before. In she came, across the room, and deposited it proudly on the hearthrug. Charles told her how clever she was. I assured her it was beautiful. Even Seeley came and sniffed it appraisingly.

A scruffy scrap of wool with a bell on it. Our visitors regarded it with amazement. 'I thought it was one of the Crown Jewels at least,' said one of them after a pause. In this house it was, I said, gathering it up and locking it for safety in the bureau.

Twelve

WE WERE A LOT more careful after that, letting her have her ball only when we were around to see where she put it. Howl though she might, it was hers only at strictly specified times, one of which was nine o'clock at night.

She quickly learned the routine. Up till then she might be doing anything – blissfully on her back warming her stomach before the fire, helping Charles with his painting, tormenting Seeley... on the stroke of nine, just as Sheba had been with the milk, Shebalu was on the bureau insistently demanding her ball. It was her Right, we understood, to have it Now. Under her Siamese Charter.

Shebalu's charter covered a lot of things. Seeley, for instance, wasn't allowed to snore. If he did, whether he was on my lap or dreaming under his rug, Shebalu went up and peremptorily poked him. It was the funniest thing to see him embarrassedly open one eye and stop – Seeley, who could have flattened her with a paw. He doted on her so much it was really quite incredible and he demonstrated it in so many ways. Sometimes I tried to get him to play with the ball with the bell. It had been his as a kitten and there was no reason why they shouldn't share it. He'd just pat it gently and look at Shebalu, who needed no second invitation to move in and take it. Even more remarkable, on several occasions when I threw it to him on the settee, he picked it up in his mouth and dropped it deliberately over the edge – to where his cross-eyed girlfriend waited confidently below.

Instead of her imitating him, too, Seeley was now copying her. If she sat on the table watching Charles at work on a painting – Seeley was up there earnestly watching as well. If she drank the paint-water, which she very often did, being thirsty from so much talking – then Seeley must have his turn. Once, when she kept trying to drink a particularly poisonous-looking jar of paint-water. Charles went out to change it, came back with a clean lot – and found that Seeley. determined to keep his end up, had eaten all the paint off his palette. Prussian Blue, Burnt Sienna and Gamboge. Seeley was perfectly all right but Charles's ulcer played him up all night, worrying about the paint in Seeley's stomach.

Seeley even moved at the same pace that she did. Shebalu went everywhere at the double and came down the stairs like tumbleweed. Beside her, always, was Seeley. His head turned towards her, his long legs performing a sort of rocking-horse canter as he checked his stride to match her gait – he looked for all the world like a trainer pacing a runner. One could imagine him quite easily in a striped jersey. Only in this case the runner, small, determined and boss-eyed, was always eventually allowed to win.

It was such a peaceful time, after the upset of losing Solomon and Sheba – like coming into harbour after a very stormy passage. He'd been thinking, said Charles, as we sat by the fire one night, Seeley on my lap, Shebalu on his and Annabel contentedly eating out in her stable... here we were, everything going so well, what about putting in the plans for the cottage extension?

This was something we'd had in mind for a long time. Originally ours had been a typical West Country cottage – small, whitewashed, red-tiled, with two rooms up, two down and a lean-to cartshed at the back. The previous owners had knocked the two downstairs rooms into one and built a kitchen and bathroom in place of the cartshed. We had added on an entrance hall at the side so that one didn't step straight into the sitting room, and there was a greenhouse and a conservatory, a garage at the top of the garden, and a stable for Annabel across the way. We didn't need much more room, we said. Except that it *would* be nice to have the bathroom upstairs, so that people didn't have to wander through the sitting room in their dressing gowns. And if we had that, of course, we could knock the old bathroom and passage into the sitting room and make a dining area, which would also be very useful. And while we were building on a bathroom upstairs, over the existing bathroom, we might as well have a room over the kitchen as well... we really *could* do with a study.

We could indeed, seeing that our one small spare room was crammed with papers, books, Charles's easel, my typewriter, our canoe sails, a piano (so that

I could practise in the necessary seclusion) and, if we happened to be going out, two cat-boxes in case they were needed. When, we had people staying, everything, with the exception of the piano which weighed about half a ton, had to be moved into our bedroom. What with having to keep their belongings on the piano, trek downstairs to the loo and, if we happened to open our bedroom door when they were passing, an easel was likely to fall out and narrowly miss them... sometimes, though they were our friends, they looked definitely bemused.

Our bathroom fittings were old-fashioned, too. We had a bath like a horse-trough and a lavatory with a high cistern and a very long chain which was always coming off in visitors' hands. How out-of-date it was had been brought home to us some while before when a cousin from Saskatchewan, visiting us for the first time ever, went into the bathroom. A while later he emerged, rushed to find his wife who was standing out on the lawn and, his face shining with excitement, said 'Nellie! You should come and see! They've got one of those that you *pull*!' Nellie, profoundly impressed, accompanied him hotfoot to see this relic of old England. On the Saskatchewan prairies, it seems, they have low-flush suites and central heating. Not a little house beside a log-pile with a moose calling behind it, as I had romantically imagined.

One way and another it was obviously time we carried out the alterations. We'd put it off for years, what with the mess we knew it would involve and not wanting to upset the cats. Solomon and Sheba were ageing and the hammering and knocking down of walls would have

115

disturbed them. Solomon, in particular, was a very nervous cat. He'd have gone round being haunted for weeks.

Now, however, we had two young cats with nerves of iron and constitutions to match. And if I wilted a little at the prospect of all the rubble – just think, said Charles, how nice it would be when we had all that extra space.

So Charles embarked on the plans, which he'd decided to draw up himself, and the cats sat interestedly on the table and watched him and I thought thoughts of my own. Charles was talking of doing some of the alterations himself. The painting, he said. Maybe some of the woodwork. Certainly he could move out all the rubble... At which stage I produced my own proposition. I thought I'd learn to drive, I said.

Charles couldn't have been more alarmed if I'd said I was going to learn to fly. Years before he'd given me driving lessons himself, and they hadn't been much of a success. For a start I couldn't reverse. True I'd only tried it once... when I'd been turning across a country road and a petrol tanker had come along, revving impatiently at us to pass, and Charles, embarrassed because we were holding it up, had said 'Back! Quick now! Back into that gate!' He was even more embarrassed when I did. *He* hadn't had to be shown how to reverse, said Charles, while the tanker-driver drove ecstatically on. He'd done it automatically. Three lessons he'd had before he'd gone out on his own and how I'd managed to knock down that gatepost...

I heard quite often about Charles's three lessons. When he said 'Pull in for those sheep' and I ran the car up a bank. When I passed another car and he thought I shouldn't have done. Whenever I tried to start our car on a hill.

He'd never had any difficulty said Charles as we rolled inexorably backwards. He just couldn't understand it. For heaven's sake why didn't I let in the CLUTCH!

It was over a hill-start that my lessons came to an abrupt conclusion. There we were approaching a country crossroads, on an uphill gradient, nothing else at all in sight. 'Stop,' said Charles. 'Look right... look left... look right again... NOW you move out carefully... gently in with the clutch...' The inevitable happened. We went backwards. And, just as inevitably, when I did as Charles said and let in the clutch, we jerked as if we'd been suddenly lassoed, went forward in a series of jumps like a kangaroo – and stopped with a sickening thump.

After that I couldn't start the engine. There was too much petrol in the carburettor. And it was all right for Charles... his legs were so long... mine, sloping uphill, barely reached the pedals. Backwards we rolled, forwards we jumped – and by this time we were no longer alone. Buses to the right of us, lorries to the left of us, a stream of traffic behind us, all held up by me.

People were looking at us, said Charles. (Boy, was that an understatement!) Why on earth didn't I get it *moving*! (I hauled fruitlessly on the starter again.) He'd never had this trouble said Charles, and he'd only had three lessons. Where was I going? he asked as I got out of the car.

'To have some blasted lessons!' I said as I marched off round the corner... where, before about fifty interested spectators, I sat down on the bank and jammed my elbows on my knees.

This isn't unusual, of course. There are probably dozens of learner-driver wives fuming by roadsides at this very moment while their husbands get their cars out of jams. Not so long ago a friend of mine, now an excellent driver, told me what happened to her when she was practising up for her test.

Almost ready for it she was, she said – though of course her husband didn't think so. And there they were, driving along, and he'd said 'When I say stop, you *stop*'... an emergency stop she thought he meant; she'd been practising on that. So when he said 'Stop!' she slammed on the brakes, tremendously pleased with her reaction – and he, poor man, having merely meant there was a junction ahead, knocked himself silly on the windscreen.

He was furious when he came round, she said, which she thought was most unreasonable. She'd got out of the car and walked all the way home, with him driving along behind her. Six miles, she said, roaring at the memory, pleading every few yards for her to get in – and her saying she'd never set foot in his old car again until she'd passed her test.

Six lessons at a driving school and she passed all right, and her husband was thrilled to bits. I bet he'd be, too, I said to Charles, when I could drive him in an emergency. 'What emergency?' asked Charles suspiciously. Well – if his ulcer blew up, I said... or he broke his leg or anything, working on the building...

'Thanks very much,' said Charles. From the way he spoke you'd think I intended personally pushing him off the scaffolding. The trouble with men is that they don't face up to things. The time in fact did come...

But that is jumping ahead of events. He relaxed a little when he found I didn't intend learning in our car.

I wouldn't be touching it for ages, I assured him. He relaxed even more when, meeting me from my first lesson, he found I'd brought the driving school car back in one piece.

'Do you think she'll be all right?' he asked the instructress.

Did she hesitate as she said 'Yes'?

Thirteen

I'D PICKED MISS PRINCE as my instructress for two reasons. She had a reputation as a first-class teacher, and she operated from a village three miles from where we lived. If, as seemed likely, it was going to take me months to learn, I preferred that nobody locally should know what I was doing.

I might as well not have bothered, of course. If I'd taken driving lessons in Timbuctoo, somebody from the village would have turned up by the next plane. I managed just two lessons incognito in Briddar... crawling cautiously around its narrow streets, stopping dead with alarm when anything came towards me... and on my third time out, there was Father Adams, coming as large as life out of a shop.

I hoped he wouldn't see me. He always wore his trilby so far down over his eyes it was a wonder he could see anything. It was hardly likely, either, that he'd expect me to be in a driving school car. Furthermore I was in disguise. I don't wear glasses in the normal way but I'd got some, being short sighted, for driving. With big tortoiseshell frames behind which, with any luck, he wouldn't recognise me in a month of Sundays.

He did of course. I had a feeling at the time that it was a bit overdone, the way he stood on the edge of the pavement, gazed hard up the street towards the village cross, hard in the other direction towards the supermarket, and apparently didn't for one moment notice that there was a car right under his nose. Sure enough, up he came that very evening and questioned Charles in his usual tactful way. 'Whass she doin' – learnin' to drive?' he asked. (I hardly supposed I looked as if I was flying.) 'Think she'll make it?' I heard him enquire. I didn't hear Charles's reply.

He is an old friend of ours, however, and once Charles had explained matters – particularly when Charles said people were so inquisitive and Father Adams commented 'Ah, specially old Mother Wellington'... once he envisaged this as a plot to keep it from her... followed later by the triumphant moment when Miss Wellington would say fancy me having learned to drive and he could say he knowed about it all along... once all that had passed before his vision we had full co-operation from Father Adams. He didn't even admit to me that he knew what I was up to. Just looked knowing whenever we met and, when he saw me again in Briddar, gazed even harder in the opposite direction.

Unfortunately he wasn't the only one who saw me. It so happened that there was a shop in Briddar – I hadn't known this before – which sold a special type of working trouser. A sort of brick-coloured heavy twill which was apparently all the local rage. All the village men were wearing them and you couldn't get them anywhere else. That was what Father Adams had been buying when I saw him that day on the pavement... and once Ern Biggs saw Father Adams in his natty brick-coloured trousers, Ern was over in Briddar like lightning after a pair for himself.

It was inevitable, of course. Since I was circling round Briddar on my lessons like a particularly determined driver on the Dodgems, Ern only had to be there buying his trousers and he was absolutely bound to see me. He did too. Coming out of the very same shop. And there was no pretending he hadn't noticed me. He stood on the pavement and gawked. Neither did he keep quiet about it. It was his big item of news for days. I only had to pass him, chatting at somebody's gate, and I knew what the conversation would be about. How he'd had to jump for his life... probably that everybody else had, too... 'Goggles like ruddy gert telescopes' I heard him say on one occasion.

So, my plans for keeping it a secret thwarted, on I drove; only too thankful that Ern Biggs wasn't around on other occasions. When I crashed the gears, for instance, or went remorselessly backwards down hills; or the occasion on which I drove the car straight onto the pavement in Briddar High Street.

I bet there aren't many learners whose instructors tell them on their fourth lesson out 'On to the pavement! Quick!' I said so to Miss Prince as we sat in the car on it afterwards. She said it wasn't normally part of the instruction. I shouldn't make a habit of it. But she said… when you had a van unloading outside a shop on the opposite side of the road and from behind that van, as one approached it, came a lorry going far too fast to stop… on to the pavement was the only thing if one didn't want to swop the car for a harp.

Charles nearly dropped when I told him. It could only happen to me, he said. That was what Miss Prince said, too, I admitted. Thank heaven Ern Biggs hadn't been around.

So I plodded on behind my L-plates, while Charles got on with the extension plans. I hoped to take my test in the Spring, which was when he intended the alterations should start. Just in time, I secretly thought, if he was going to do any of the work himself.

He said he was. More and more he said so as on the one hand we heard how building costs were rising and, on the other, of people undertaking the work themselves. After talking to someone in the village who'd done his own extension completely, Charles even saw us doing the block-laying. In gay Norwegian sweaters, he said. Presumably to give that nonchalant effect.

This, however, was November. It was a long time yet to the Spring. Christmas came first, with log fires and family parties, and building and driving lessons forgotten.

It passed peacefully enough, save for one or two minor incidents. Seeley went off his food on Christmas night, for instance, which had me worried till I realised he was still full of beans. Doing his act up the bathroom door and going round chairs on his back.

A while later, in the kitchen, I opened the refrigerator door and Seeley appeared silently behind me. Shebalu was in the sitting room, joining in the party games.

While we two were on our own, Seeley's gaze intimated... Surely I knew what he Wanted? I should have done. Seeley, as a kitten, had been brought up on turkey and chicken... before we had him, that was, but it was something he'd never forgotten. Now there was one in the refrigerator, reminding him of his childhood. He stretched out his head towards it, sniffing, in case I thought he meant the sausages...

He got it, of course. He ate turkey rapturously for days. Shebalu couldn't have cared less. That stuff *again*, she said, shaking her leg at it. Didn't we have any rabbit?

Not that she was unimpressed by Christmas. Eyes round as saucers from the moment she got up, she was forever trying to reach the holly or climbing the Christmas tree. Any time we have had a Christmas tree there have always been cats in the branches. Now there was a new little cat. I looked at her, and remembered...

She also ate all the flowers off an indoor chrysanthemum. Twelve brilliant yellow blooms it had, and was a present from a friend. I'd put it on the hall chest, which showed it off to perfection. The next time I saw it, it didn't have a flower on it. Just a few scattered petals around from which you could tell what colour it had been.

It was Seeley, she said when I carried her out and confronted her with it. If I asked her, he'd gone a bit funny through eating all that turkey. It wasn't Seeley, of course; I knew that very well. Half an hour later I caught her eating the leaves.

Siamese, on principle, always misbehave at Christmas. Whether it's the competition – so many visitors they feel it necessary to outshine. Whether it's the atmosphere – all the excitement and laughter and general air of laissez-faire. Whether it's the relaxation of supervision and with Siamese one should never relax...

Just after Christmas I had a letter from a friend who had two Siamese. Sheba (after our old girl) and her adopted brother Igor. She bet we couldn't guess what they'd done this year, she said. She was right. We certainly couldn't.

Apparently she'd given a party for which, among other things, she'd made some cream meringues. Knowing that pair, she said, she'd wanted to lock them (the cats) in the bedroom. If she'd suggested putting them in chains in a dungeon, however, her husband couldn't have been more appalled. So they'd been allowed to join in the party, adding tone to it as only Siamese can. She'd kept a weather eye on them, of course. They'd just eyed her innocently back. Until, she said, she'd brought in a heavy tray and hadn't been able to close the door behind her... and a few minutes later she noticed that Sheba had vanished.

She was after her in an instant, frantically fearing the worst. Everything seemed all right, however. The meringues were still on their dish on the kitchen dresser. Sheba was sitting thinking on the landing upstairs. Even when she picked up the meringues a little later and found there wasn't any cream in them she couldn't be sure she wasn't at fault. They looked so untouched, she wondered if she was going crackers. She supposed she *had* put in the cream?

She got her answer on Boxing Day when Sheba had diarrhoea like a tap. It would peter out if it had been caused by cream, the Vet said when she called him. But if she liked he'd come over and give the sufferer something to make sure... It was cream all right. By five o'clock the culprit was bawling for her food and pulling

James the spaniel's ears. Only, wrote Mia, no sooner had she got over that fright, than Igor nearly did for her for good and all.

The previous week she and her husband had bought an electric log fire – just for effect, as they had central heating. They only used the log part – never the fire – though after half an hour or so the logs, which had a bulb inside, did get slightly warm. Anyway, she rang the Vet to tell him it had been the cream with Sheba, came back into the sitting room, her mind on something else – and there lay Igor on top of the logs, artificial flames all round him, and for a moment she forgot that they weren't real. It looked so horrible, she said, she nearly fainted. Just like one of the Old Testament stories with Igor as the sacrificial lamb. And then that horrible cat opened his eyes and smirked at her. Nice spot to relax on, he said.

The owners of Spice and Sugar had also been having trouble. We heard from Dora over the phone. She was sorry about her voice sounding so peculiar, she said. It was a wonder she had a voice at all...

The previous night, it seemed, they too had had visitors and the cats had been allowed to join in. (Better than locking them in her bedroom, said Dora. Last time Spice had taken down the cornices. Polystyrene, she said... Yes, she knew cats could get their claws in it but she thought it would have been safe enough on the *ceiling*...) Anyway, when it was going home time they did shut the cats in the bedrooms. Sugar in Nita's room, Spice in hers, so they couldn't march out with the visitors. Past twelve o'clock it was and when she opened her bedroom door and found that Spice had gone... out through the transom window, which she hadn't realised was open... the one consolation was that it was raining.

Spice didn't like the rain. She couldn't be far, thought Dora. One discreet little call, not to disturb the neighbours, and she'd be back like a greyhound, yelling to be wiped.

Come one o'clock and, after a good many discreet little calls, Spice still wasn't home. Come two o'clock and the discreet little calls had been abandoned. She and Nita were up at a nearby market garden, shouting over the walls like mad. In people's gardens, down an electricity trench... they were building several more bungalows along at the end of the road and Nita, in the dark, went round every one. It was pouring with rain. Their hair-do's, done specially for the previous evening's party, were hanging down their foreheads like seaweed. Still there was no Spice – and now they were beginning to think it was hopeless. If she were alive, she'd never be out in weather like that.

At three o'clock they went to bed. Not to sleep, said Nora. Jut to lie down because they were so exhausted. At five they were up and out again, roaming the streets with torches. She wasn't calling now, said Dora. Her voice had gone and anyway she was no longer expecting any answer. All she expected was to find a sad little bundle lying somewhere in the gutter... caught by a car or a late-roaming dog, lying there soaked by the ram...

She was on her way up to the old quarry – a wild place, all hummocks and stunted bushes. Not that she'd ever known Spice go as far as that – but she must, thought Dora, have gone *somewhere*.

She had. And on her way to the quarry Dora met her coming back from it. She thought she saw something slipping past, elusively, at a distance – and when she whispered 'Spice?' the shadow answered.

She was scared, said Dora. She was soaked. Where she'd been for all those hours they'd never know. Only that Spice was now full of beans and showing off to Sugar, while Dora thought she'd probably caught flu.

Gosh, I could imagine how she'd worried, I said to Charles. Remember the time Sheba was missing all night? When Father Adams had been going to dig out a fox-earth because we thought there was no place else she could be? And the hundreds of miles we must have run looking for Solomon, said Charles. Remember the time we'd missed two trains to London?

I did indeed. Both of them had been involved in that. I could see us now, running round the lanes like agitated ants, me frantically shrilling 'Teeby-teeby-teeby' and 'Solly-wolly-wolly' and Charles, who is much more dignified, clucking. I remembered the feeling of relief when, with half-an-hour to spare, Charles located them sitting inside a thorn thicket. We couldn't get in to them but at least we knew where they were. If we waited a minute or two, we thought, they'd be coming out to join us.

An hour and a half later we were still waiting. The only difference was, Charles having fetched the shears to cut a way into them, they were now sitting further inside the thicket. Weren't coming, said Solomon. They knew where we were Going. Off all day, said Sheba. Leaving them on their Own.

Eventually we'd given it up. 'We'd better send a telegram to say we're not coming,' I said. 'Or get them to broadcast a message on Paddington Station.' Walking defeatedly back to the cottage we looked back up the track and there they were following behind. Sheba in front, Solomon trotting at her heels... angelic now they thought they'd gained their purpose.

They hadn't. We caught a later train. Neither did they spend the time moping. As soon as our backs were turned, as well we knew, they'd be chasing round the cottage over the furniture. So many times we'd come back for something we'd forgotten and caught them tearing about. Very sheepish they'd looked, too, when we walked in on them. Thought we'd Gone, said the expressions on their faces.

I remembered, I said. And if I felt a pang of sadness, as one does for things that are past... 'At least we don't have to worry about those two,' I said. 'They don't go off like that.'

Once again I was wrong. Within weeks we were worrying like mad.

Fourteen

IT WAS THE SPRING, of course, and the fact that Shebalu
was growing up. She still played with her ball with a
bell on and Seeley – at times, anyway – still acted as
though he were her grandfather. She was too big now
to get under the armchair, though – where, pretending
she was a mouse he'd lost, he used to corner her and
refuse to let her come out. And once or twice they'd
appeared playing boys and girls together, a sure sign she
was growing up.

'Appeared' is the only word for it. Like Solomon and
Sheba before them, they invariably did it in public. As on
the occasion when some neighbours were asking after
Shebalu and I said I'd give her a shout. 'Doo-doo-doo-
doo' I called – feeling foolish even as I did it. I couldn't
yodel 'Shebalu', however, and 'Teeby-teeby' was too like
'Seeley' – so Doodoo she'd become for calling purposes,
on account of the Lu at the end, and she always answered

instantly, like a retriever to a whistle. She came tearing round the corner now – a flurry of blue and white fur and long legs. With her, as usual, was Seeley. 'They're terrific friends,' I said.

They made that obvious all right. Seeley, following behind her, suddenly jumped on Shebalu's back. She dropped, squealing but patently enjoying it, flat on her stomach on the ground. He, holding her in a cave-cat grip by the back of her neck, yowled triumphantly through her fur. And thus, for all the world to see, they advanced towards us up the path. 'Are you going to breed with them?' our neighbours asked. They were most surprised when I said it wasn't possible.

At least they'd come when they were called, however, and they did arrive together. The morning came when I went out to summon them for breakfast and there was no Shebalu in sight. 'Doo-doo-doo-doo' I called enticingly – but only Seeley arrived. Scurrying round the corner like a tracker dog, looking worriedly about him as he came. He'd lost her. She'd vanished while his back was turned. Had we found her? he said.

An hour later, when we were almost on our knees with searching, she suddenly erupted out of the forest. Tearing top speed down the hill from the pine trees, telling us how exciting it was in there. It must have been, too – all those tall avenues of trees, and the pine needles to walk on and the silence all around her. And the foxes, we told her. We'd heard their mating calls in the night. She was city-bred. What could she know of foxes?

I felt happier when I saw her practising climbing. Going like a squirrel up one of the pine trees behind the cottage – then down and up the next one, with Seeley exuberantly in her wake. He fell off as soon as he got a few feet up, but obviously nothing would ever catch her. Charles, though, with whom she'd taken Sheba's place, firmly refused to believe it.

Now she'd discovered the forest she vanished into it every morning – and Charles, as soon as he found she was missing, always started to worry. 'You'd better call her,' he'd say. 'She'll only come to you.' And there I'd stand, hooting 'Doo-doo-doo-doo' and feeling an absolute fool...

For one thing this always produced Seeley. Whether it was that he, too, was looking for Shebalu and wanted to be on hand when she arrived, or whether he thought I was calling him, since for so long he'd come running with her when I called – 'Doo-doo-doo-doo' now became his signal call as well and he answered it more readily than 'Seeley'.

It was the impression it gave to onlookers, however. – 'Doo-doo-doo-doo' – I hadn't realised it at first – sounded exactly like a hunting horn. And when I stood in the lane and did that, and first a big seal-point came bounding up and noisily greeted me (but, to the observers' surprise, I still called on)... and then a shaggy donkey came galloping across the hillside and Woo-hoo-hooed at me over the fence... and eventually, if they waited long enough, a lone-legged kitten with fantastically crossed eyes came tearing down the hillside out of the pine trees... 'Well,' I heard the comment on one occasion. 'I aint seen nuthin' like that.'

It was a good thing Em Biggs wasn't around when they said it. He'd have told them a thing or two.

It was worth the embarrassment, though, when Shebalu did turn up; and meantime something most interesting happened. Seeley became a tracker cat.

I used to wonder about that with Solomon and Sheba – whether, when Solomon went missing, Sheba could have found him for us if she'd been so inclined. Did *she* know when he was merely behind the conservatory, or had gone off on one of his lengthy treks? If she did, she did nothing about it. We always had to find him for ourselves.

Seeley though... one day he came pelting down through Annabel's field when I was calling for Shebalu. paused against my legs to look anxiously up the Forest track, went into the yard and got on the coalhouse roof – then stood on the edge of it and pointed. There was no mistaking what he was doing. Head thrust forward, eyes narrowed he surveyed the hillside like a retriever. Looking glistening... 'Just as if!' I said. 'He couldn't hear a *kitten* in the forest!'

He did though. When he'd found the right direction he watched for a moment and then was down and speeding silently up the hillside. Into the wood he went – and sure enough, within seconds, he came out accompanied by his girlfriend.

He did it so many times that it obviously wasn't coincidence. After a while I took him with me deliberately to find her. I'd put him down at the edge of the wood. He'd look and listen, and then go trotting off. Once I thought he'd made a mistake – he went into the undergrowth on my left while she appeared, a few moments later, coming straight towards me from a track ahead. Behind her, though, like a sheepdog, came Seeley.

He'd gone in and circled round behind her. Now he was flushing her out.

And why shouldn't a cat be good at tracking? Or, if it comes to that, a donkey? Annabel often told us when one or other of them was in her field. Head down, ears pointed like antennae in their direction, watching them from under her fringe with a benevolent pout on her lips. At least, we hoped it was benevolent. One night the cats were around when I went to put Annabel into her stable.

It was raining so, not knowing what else to do, they followed us up through the garden. Into the stable they marched, where Annabel was eating maize from her bowl. She paused for a moment, looked at them and snorted. Completely ignoring her they started looking round for mice... which, they decided, after a quick survey of the walls, were definitely, without doubt, in her hay.

The hay was right by her back legs. Annabel always liked it there. So she could turn round when she'd finished her first course and continue her supper without stopping.

They sniffed, prowled, looked like a couple of Maigrets intently searching for clues... obviously only to annoy her; there probably wasn't a mouse within miles. Annabel, growing irritated, stamped backwards into the hay. Seeley, mrr-mrring in protest, took off to safety on the wall. But where, I panicked, was Shebalu? She'd completely disappeared!

Just in time, as Annabel turned towards it, I saw a movement in the hay. Shebalu was hiding inside it.

Completely invisible, so she thought, and tremendously pleased with herself. Annabel snorted again as I lifted her out. Pity I'd done that, she said, wobbling her underlip even harder. Some young cats needed teaching a lesson. She'd just been going to eat her...

Again, though – would she have hurt her, or were the three of them playing? Next morning, it still being raining, they went up to see her again. Charles saw them go in deliberately, squeezing under the bottom of her door. Charles also heard Annabel snort and stamp – and was running hard to the rescue when the cats appeared again. Grumpy in the mornings, wasn't she? they said as they strolled unconcernedly off.

Within minutes they were being chased by Nero and that didn't seem to worry them either. Down the hill from the village they streaked – we hadn't even seen them go up there. Seeley came flying over the front gatepost. Shebalu, ears flat and obviously enjoying it, rushed on into the forest and up the nearest tree... so fast we just stood there with our mouths open watching, while Nero, defeated, trotted home.

Shebalu was so fast we began to think she *liked* being chased and went out of her way to invite it. A day or so later she appeared with a ginger torn in pursuit and she certainly wasn't worried about him. I was weeding a flower-bed when I heard the scuffling of feet and she came careering on to the lawn. Not fast this time – what with horses would be called a controlled canter; head up, bounding joyously as she came. And behind her was the reddest ginger cat I've ever seen, though there was nothing controlled about him. More like the wolf after Red Riding Hood he looked, until he saw me and changed his course. Off he shot, like a jet-propelled streak, over the wall and up the lane.

Shebalu stood there disconsolately. They'd been going to play, she said. And where was guard cat Seeley, whom we'd last seen with her in the vegetable garden? As I went round to the kitchen he appeared from behind the cottage and joined me quietly inside. Discretion was obviously the better part of valour. Was it time for supper? he asked.

After that, of course, the ginger cat positively haunted us. Parading along the lane, crooning love-songs across in the orchard, sitting watching the cottage from up on the hill. And Shebalu sat in the window and watched for him. Why, she demanded, couldn't she go out to play? Because, though he couldn't mate with her, he might maul her and give her an abscess; that had once happened to Sheba. And because we didn't want Seeley getting into a fight, as had happened so often with Solomon. So, for the moment, we kept them under strict supervision – which wasn't made any easier by the fact that our building was at last under way.

The plans had been passed. Charles, to my vast relief, had decided against doing the work himself. I could well have seen us with a bathroom upstairs and no roof on it for years. And then, luck being with us, we'd managed to find Henry, who at that moment was looking for a job.

Henry, officially a sub-contracting bricklayer, could do just about anything. Plastering, carpentry, decorating... even cooking, we later learned. He'd been an Army Cook-Sergeant and would have become a pastry-cook after the War – only cooking fats were rationed and he couldn't see any future in it so he'd gone back to building instead.

There he was anyway – just finished sub-contracting for one builder, wanting a job to fill in... only he didn't like bothering with ordering the materials, he said, and he'd need somebody to give him a hand.

It couldn't have been better. We didn't mind ordering the materials. Charles, complete with Norwegian sweater, was only too willing to help with the labouring. Henry was ready to start immediately – and within a week he had.

He worked so fast we could hardly believe it. Up went the scaffolding, off came the outer line of tiles, on went the blocks. He came just after seven in the morning and hardly stopped till six at night. With me on the telephone ordering materials. Charles acting as builder's mate and the peculiarities of our household giving Henry sleepless nights.

That was Henry's trouble. He was a dreadful worrier. Whether the timber would come on time whether it would rain on his block work... just as he'd worried all those years ago about the cooking fat shortage and had taken up building instead. Annabel particularly worried him. He wasn't used to donkeys, he said.

Annabel, sensing this, intimidated him for all she was worth. Her field rises directly behind the cottage. She had always been able to look through the kitchen window. And now, from a point on her hillside level with the old bathroom roof only a few feet away from where he was working, Annabel stood and watched him from under her fringe. Stolidly. Unmoving. For hours.

Just as if she was a foreman, he said. Made him feel quite uncomfortable at times. And then, when he was sure she hadn't moved an inch – darn him, if she hadn't knocked down his ladder. That was a huge joke to Annabel. Teeth bared derisively, lips sucked in till they resembled a pair of castanets, she'd stand there and patently laugh at him while he picked it up and re-set it. And when he'd gone in the evening and she had the place to herself, she'd go round and push down anything moveable she could find, ready for the morning.

Eventually he learned to tie everything to the scaffolding. Came the night, however, when we had a heavy storm – the one night's rain we had in the whole time of building. We wouldn't have heard it ourselves but for the fact that the glass conservatory roof was now covered by corrugated iron sheets... to catch him if he fell off, said Henry, prepared for all eventualities.

We were woken by the rain beating on it like something out of Somerset Maugham. And then 'The timber!' said Charles, leaping frantically out of bed. The roofing timber had been delivered that morning and lay exposed on the lawn. Charles, himself no optimist, envisaged it warping if it got wet. So up we got. Switched on the outside lights. Out on to the lawn we dashed in pyjamas and macintoshes. Covering up the timber with tarpaulins and plastic sheets, with the wind whistling wetly round our ankles at two o'clock in the morning.

Henry's first words, when he arrived at seven, were that he hadn't slept a wink all night. He'd been worrying, he said, how things were with us in the storm. Oh, everything was all right, I said – we'd covered up all the timber. The rain on the corrugated iron had fortunately woken us up. Timber? said Henry. It wasn't the timber he'd been worrying about. A night's rain on that wouldn't have done it any harm. It was the new bathroom window he'd put in place and propped up to keep it steady. In the middle of the night he remembered he hadn't tied the poles, and he'd lain there imagining that donkey pushin' 'em away and the wind blowing the window down through the roof.

Henry must have had extra-sensory perception. Annabel hadn't moved the poles and the window hadn't come through the roof. But the very next day Henry asked Charles to help him lift the bathroom lintel, and Charles knocked a wall through the roof instead.

To give the picture I should explain that the old sloping roof at the back of the cottage was still in position – Henry's idea being to take off the outer line of tiles round the three edges of it, to build the shell of the extension up from there, and only when the new roof was safely on to take the rest of the old roof away from underneath.

From the level of the new bathroom window, therefore, one looked down upon the old back roof, as Charles discovered when he clambered up there holding one end of a heavy concrete lintel – on Henry's scaffolding, which, he said, sagged under him like a bow. Worse was to come. To lift the lintel to a height above the bathroom window Henry had positioned, on the sagging planking, a further single sagging plank raised up on concrete blocks.

Henry, who was used to it, went up on it like a ballet dancer. Charles, being inexperienced, went up like a lumbering elephant. He wobbled. Valiantly retaining his hold on the lintel he put out his elbow to balance himself. Just a touch against the wall, he said. How was he to know it would fall down?

Apparently the cement wasn't dry. Henry hadn't thought it necessary to tell him. All the years he'd been in the building trade, said Henry, and he'd never known anybody do that.

Well, but Charles wasn't in the building trade, I said, trying to pour oil on troubled waters. Henry, looking at the gap where his wall had been, said I didn't need to tell him that.

Fifteen

THE NEXT THING THAT happened was that Charles sprained his ankle. He'd been moving rubble from the cottage across to the orchard where he said it would be useful on the paths. Every morning before breakfast he carried up several plastic sacks full. Gosh, he felt fit, he said.

I thought I was seeing things when he strode past the window one morning carrying a consignment of rubble like Atlas and five minutes later... surely he couldn't be *limping*, I thought... not just from dumping rubble on a path?

He was. His foot had slipped over the edge, he said, and the weight of the sack had pulled him down. 'Wouldn't believe it, would you?' said Henry, looking at him in awe.

It was a massive multiple sprain and he limped like Long John Silver for weeks. Which, of course, was just when Seeley chose to go exploring on the roof.

The cats had been interested in the alterations from the moment the scaffolding went up; balance-walking round the block work, nipping in and out through the empty windows. Seeley, in fact, got out one night and went up on the scaffolding in the dark. At least, hearing a plank creak as I searched for him, I hoped that was what it was. My heart thumping madly – but if I went back for Charles, and it was Seeley he might get away... I climbed into Annabel's field, shone my torch along the supports, a plank rattled again and something took off into the darkness... It was Seeley all right but now he'd dodged up on to the hillside, and how on earth I was going to get him back...

The answer was psychology. One of the things the years have taught me is never to chase a Siamese cat. Just to hope to entice him back either by habit or curiosity, or he'll only go further away. In this case the obvious bait was the scaffolding, as he was so intrigued by that. And the habit – that, of course, was my calling 'Doo-doo'; ten o'clock at night or not. So I hauled myself up on to the scaffolding, turned the torch on myself so he could see me, and, feeling self-conscious as usual, started to yodel 'Doo-doo'.

It worked of course. He was back like a boomerang. But I did wonder why I had to do these things. Supposing someone saw me. What on earth would they think?

That wasn't Seeley's big roof adventure, though. That happened when the old roof was opened up. The new roof was on at the back, there was an opening at the top of the stairs through into the extension and the cats, consumed with curiosity, were going in there first thing every morning. They weren't allowed in after Henry arrived in case he accidentally walled them up.

This, I might say, was not so far-fetched a possibility as it sounds. They were in and out of everything like a pair of moles. Down into the cavity walls, underneath the floorboards... there was always a furry bottom wriggling backwards out of somewhere. Then one morning, just before the ceiling went up in the new section, Shebalu discovered a way through into the old roof over our bedroom. A dark, inviting hole at the top of one of the walls.

Before we could stop her she was up, through it and after the starlings. We could hear them in there twittering and scrabbling like mad – they hadn't expected an attack from the rear. Charles immediately imagined her being trapped. Chasing birds in that old lathe and plaster, he said, and there was no way for us to get in. Some minutes later she emerged again. Birdless, but covered in cobwebs. No sooner was she out, however, than Seeley promptly went in.

He came out all right, too. It was a bit like waiting for Theseus to emerge from the labyrinth... a pretty woolly headed Theseus, busily copying Shebalu as usual... but out he came all right, apart from the cobwebs. It was Exciting in there, he said.

So exciting that they took to going in there every morning, with Charles eternally forecasting they'd get stuck. How would we get them out? he asked – he with his gammy foot? How could we stop them from getting *in*? I said. We had no answer to that.

Anyway, one morning Shebalu caught a starling. We could tell that by the flapping and squawking inside the roof. And Charles was having a fit – both for the starling's safety and for his blue-pointed girlfriend.

Starlings can be nasty if they attack a cat. I called her. Never was 'Doo-doo-doo' uttered more heartfeltly. And I was answered – though oddly enough it sounded more like Seeley... except I was sure he was out. I called again, and kept being answered, and eventually Shebalu put in an appearance with a full-grown starling in her mouth.

I soon rescued him. Standing on the step-ladder, as she came through the hole I grabbed the scruff of Shebalu's neck, held it – and in seconds she'd let go of the bird. It didn't hurt or frighten her. It always works. And the bird was away in a flash. He didn't seem particularly scared, either. I could see him watching me beadily over a rafter inside the hole. Only... there was still a Siamese calling... and it wasn't Shebalu. She was now in the extension with us.

It was Seeley. 'Seeley!' I yelled in panic. 'Wooooo' came a muffled voice from the direction of the roof. I knew that note, too. I know all of Seeley's voices. Somewhere my seal-point friend was in distress. 'He's stuck!' said Charles, visualising him with his head jammed under a rafter. 'Or hurt,' I said, thinking of a starling's beak.

As a matter of fact he was neither. After a despairing moment in which Charles said why did it happen to us and I wondered if I could possibly squeeze through the hole, we pulled ourselves together and formed a plan of campaign. I was to stay where I was and keep calling to comfort him. Charles was to get a ladder round to the front of the cottage. Charles would then go up it, take off the tiles and try to find him. And if that didn't work we'd call the fire brigade.

It was a sensible plan. It probably would have worked – except that when Charles limped round the cottage with the ladder he found there was no need for it. Seeley was sitting up in the rain-water gutter looking down at him. Marooned he was, said Seeley. About time we brought that ladder. Another couple of seconds and he might have fallen off.

He hadn't been inside the roof at all. He must have got up on to the new flat roof at the back, walked down the steep-sloping roof at the front, my 'Doo-doo-doo' must have sounded as if it was coming from the guttering – and there he'd been answering me, wondering why I didn't appear. Probably he'd expected me to come out through a hole like a starling; Seeley thought I could do anything. One thing we did know, Seeley didn't have a head for heights. There was nothing for it even now, but for Charles to climb up to get him. He was going up the ladder when Henry arrived. 'Where's he off to now?' enquired Henry. 'Going to practise parachuting?' I looked at him. 'Well,' said Henry unrepentantly. 'You never know in this place.'

Things were coming along, nevertheless. The partitions went up, the plumber arrived, in next to no time the new bathroom was installed. It didn't have a door on it, of course – not for weeks. That was one of the jobs Charles was going to do.

My driving was progressing too. At least, according to Miss Prince. It wouldn't be long before I took my test, she was saying now, though when I passed that on to Charles he raised his eyes to the heavens.

The thing was, I was used to her car by this time. It was small, it had four gears, the gear stick was on the floor... and when Charles suggested I should try our car (we had to face it some time was the way he put it)... I found everything was exactly opposite. Ours was bulky, it had three gears, the gear-lever was on the steering-column. Even the indicators worked the opposite way. Down was Right on ours... it was Left on hers... I whipped them up and down as if I was playing an organ. Also, our car had a long-rising clutch pedal, while hers made contact in an instant. Let ours in fast and we jumped like a bucking cow... or else I did it too cautiously and for ages we didn't move at all.

It was always happening at junctions. 'Come on now – hurry up,' Charles would urge me, seeing nothing in sight for miles. And I'd let out the clutch and we'd leap into the road and the engine would stop and I couldn't get it started... 'I don't do this in *hers*,' I would wail. Charles said it was just as well, otherwise by this time she wouldn't have had a body on her chassis.

The biggest snag, however, was the width of our car. Even after I got over stopping it dead when anything came towards me on the wide roads I still wouldn't take it round narrow lanes. Certainly I wouldn't drive it from the main road down to the cottage. Our lane winds exceptionally and there are a couple of nasty corners – and anyway I didn't want anybody to see me. Ern might have told everyone I was a learner, but there was no need for them to actually see me at it.

One night, though, after I'd done quite a trouble-free journey out from town... only a couple of clutch-jumps this time, said Charles; we'd make a driver out of me yet... he suggested I did take it all the way home. There wouldn't be much traffic, he said, and nobody'd know it was me in the dark and at some time or other I had to try it out...

Poor Charles. He was trying to encourage me. Round the first corner I rolled – absolutely nothing in sight. Towards the second bend... I could see car headlights coming round it. 'Slow down!' said Charles. It was all right; I already had. I'd pulled towards a gateway as a matter of fact and stopped to let the other car go through. 'I only said Slow,' said Charles. 'No need to *stop*.' So obediently I went on – which was when I hit the wall.

Touched it actually. It was Charles who said I'd scraped it and, jamming on the hand-brake, leapt out and rushed to take over in the driving seat. He avoided looking at the wing. He said he couldn't.

When I got home I looked at it and there was one minute scratch on the bumper. Charles, agreeing that perhaps he could polish it out, said it *could* have buckled the wing though. It didn't make much difference that it hadn't, he said. It was avoidance of the object that counted.

Not for the first time I wondered whether it was possible to win. It was though. The time came when Charles admitted I wasn't driving too badly. It was fortunate I could, he said, even with L-plates, when he'd damaged his foot carrying the rubble. And the extension was nearly complete... everything was falling into place. It promised to be a wonderful Spring, too – Shebalu's first with us ever. I spent a lot of time with her and Seeley up on the hillside, watching over them on account of adders and enjoying, with them, their youth.

We were up there the morning the extension literally did fall into place. The downstairs part was nearly finished now. The old bathroom had been removed and the wall had been taken away, huge jacks supporting the ceiling while it was done. They'd stayed there while four enormous lintels had been cemented into place, and for three days more while it set. That very morning the jacks had been removed and Henry had actually smiled. The place had stayed up after all then, he said. Had I checked that the chimney pots were still on?

That wasn't what I was doing on the hillside. Charles, that morning, had reported seeing Seeley chasing a mouse at the foot of a tree. And later that he'd chased it up the tree, and caught it and brought it down. Then he'd lost it, and the mouse had run up the tree again, and Seeley had once more climbed up after it...

Well, a mouse ran up a clock in the nursery-rhyme so there was no reason why it shouldn't go up a tree... or that Seeley, our seal-point clown, shouldn't go up the tree after it. But for the mouse to run up the tree a second time – did it perhaps have its home up there?

That was what I was investigating when I heard the crash which sounded as if the cottage staircase had collapsed. I rushed from one direction, Charles from another, and we converged, white as sheets, in the sitting room. It wasn't the staircase – and Henry hadn't been flattened, as we'd feared. One of the ceiling beams had fallen down.

It was quite simple. The beams, which were false, were supported at either end on decorative brackets. Henry, in removing part of the wall, had removed the bracket from under one end of a beam. He'd supported the beam with a prop, removed the prop when he took away the jacks – and, with nothing to support it, the beam had simply collapsed. Not immediately. The ceiling-plaster had held it to the ceiling. Until, half-an-hour later, its weight brought it thundering down.

One end lay on an armchair, the other on the floor... it was so heavy the three of us could scarcely lift it Why hadn't we told him it wasn't screwed to the joists? said Henry. The answer was that we hadn't known. Charles was absolutely appalled. All these years people had been sitting in that chair, and at any moment the beam could have come down. Only those brackets supporting it... he'd have to see to them at once. He wouldn't rest until all the beams were screwed to the joists.

'Twas all right for him to talk about resting. said Henry. He'd nearly gone to his. He'd been bending down doing a bit of plastering when the thing had come down and it had missed his backside by inches. He was beginning to wonder, he said, what next was going to happen.

Sixteen

NOTHING, AS A MATTER of fact. We are back to the peaceful calm of when we started. Annabel is grazing out on the hillside and Jane Robart has just ridden past. Still with the air of Elizabeth the First graciously patronising the peasants. 'Ought to let thy donkey loose,' Ern Biggs said the other day. 'Bet he'd put the wind up her.'

'She,' I corrected him. 'Annabel.' Ern still gets everything wrong. 'As a matter of fact she did, last year.'

'Did she now?' said Ern. 'How was that, then?' Father Adams superiorly told him.

That is the one thing the year has brought – those two now speak to each other. Each one trying to score, of course, as countrymen always do. Both of them bait Miss Wellington, too – and for all her indignation she enjoys it. She is up in her garden now, wearing the headgear she considers appropriate to the season. 'Well, summer's here then,' Father

150

Adams always says. 'Old Ma Wellington's out in her straw hat.'

Ern Biggs' eyes nearly jumped out when he saw it first, with its steeple-shaped crown and raffia flowers. 'Whass she got on? A beehive?' he enquired. Father Adams was quick to correct him. 'Just shows thee ignorance – thass her *hat*,' he roared. 'She bin wearin' he for nigh on forty years.'

Probably she has, too – though that was long before we came to the village. Things don't change much in the country. Our extension is finished – we hadn't got that a year ago – but you'd hardly notice it from the front. 'Looks just the same as it ever did,' says Father Adams. 'Ah – and thee grass still wants cuttin',' says Ern.

My driving lessons have been something new, of course, but once I pass my test even that will be taken for granted. It's only being a learner that arouses comment. As Charles says – And how! He had the brakes done last week. I said I hoped it wasn't my fault. He couldn't blame that on my going through a pothole or too near a wall? Charles grinned and admitted that he couldn't. The thing we didn't know, of course, was that in adjusting the brakes the mechanic somehow mis-aligned the braking lights. As soon as the engine was switched on, whatever the car was doing, the braking lights were on. The stranger who stopped us and told us about it miles from home, realised something was wrong – he could understand the lights being on going downhill. he said – but not when we were going uphill as well.

They didn't realise it here – or they pretended they didn't. Being so near my test I am now driving openly through the village with L-plates, getting used to the lane.

So it was that when I was seen driving our car up the hill with the braking lights resplendently on – 'How'd she manage that then?' Ern enquired interestedly later of Charles. 'I've never seen anybody doin' that before.'

'Spec thass what they teaches 'em nowadays in these schools,' said Father Adams. 'With women they probably wants to be double sure.'

They are a pair of old rapscallions and they know it – but we wouldn't change them one bit. Part of the joy of country life is its affectionate gossip and banter. And for us it is also two Siamese cats, sitting up on the hillside. A little blue-point batting flies; a big seal-point proudly watching her; and nearby, a donkey grazing and surreptitiously eyeing the pair of them. Just as it has been now for so many years and yet might easily not have been. If we'd mourned Solomon and Sheba so much that we'd decided not to replace them.

Replace them, I say... Seeley is so much like Solomon that it might easily be him. Sometimes I forget for a moment and it *is* Solomon who races down the hillside, jumps on to my shoulder and rubs his face against mine to show how he loves me. Certainly he reminded me of Solomon when I put Annabel in the other night. Seeley had been hanging round waiting for his supper and had presumably forgotten the time of day. When I came out of the kitchen with Annabel's water-bucket he thought I was bringing out his breakfast. That, after all is the usual procedure – he waits at the back door, I come out carrying the saucer and we march in procession to the conservatory.

We went in procession this time, too. I carrying the water-bucket, Seeley accompanying me, mrr-mrring and anxiously looking up at it... straight into the conservatory where he looked back to see if I was following. If that wasn't like Solomon, I said to Charles, thinking his supper was in the bucket... a couple of bat-brains if ever I'd seen them; he and Seeley both.

Lovable bat-brains. And though Shebalu is completely different from Sheba, she is lovable too. Long-headed and Roman-nosed, where Sheba was round-faced and flat-nosed... but very beautiful, and as much a part of the place as we are ourselves. Shebalu and her ball with the bell on, and her addiction to washing up mops.

She is going off into the woods now, with Seeley close behind her. As we hope they will be for many years to come.

CATS
IN THE BELFRY

'The most enchanting cat book ever'
Jilly Cooper

DOREEN TOVEY

CATS IN THE BELFRY

Doreen Tovey

£6.99
Paperback

ISBN 10: 1 84024 452 6
ISBN 13: 978 1 84024 452 6

'It wasn't, we discovered as the months went by, that Sugieh was particularly wicked. It was just that she was a Siamese.'

Animal lover Doreen and her husband Charles acquire their first Siamese kitten to rid themselves of an invasion of mice. But Sugieh is not just any cat. She's an actress, a prima donna, an iron hand in a delicate, blue-pointed glove. She quickly establishes herself as queen of the house, causing chaos daily by screaming like a banshee, chewing up telegrams, and tearing holes in anything made of wool.

First published over forty years ago, this warm and witty classic tale is a truly enjoyable read for anyone who's ever been owned by a cat.

CATS
IN MAY

From the bestselling author of
Cats In The Belfry

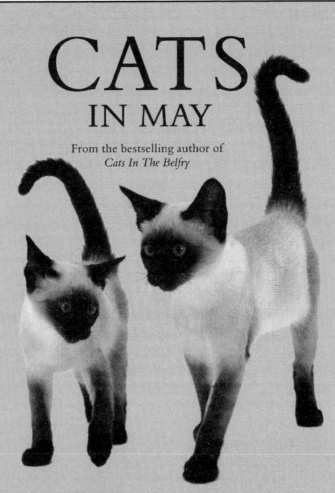

DOREEN TOVEY

CATS IN MAY

Doreen Tovey

£6.99
Paperback

ISBN 10: 1 84024 497 6
ISBN 13: 978 1 84024 497 7

'All our animals showed their independence at a dishearteningly early age.'

The Toveys attempt to settle down to a quiet life in the country. Unfortunately for them, however, their tyrannical Siamese cats have other ideas.

From causing an uproar on the BBC to staying out all night and claiming to have been kidnapped, Sheba and Solomon's outrageous behaviour leaves the Toveys at their wits' end. Meanwhile Doreen has to contend with her husband's disastrous skills as a handyman, and a runaway tortoise called Tarzan.

Both human and animal characters come to life on the page, including Sidney the problem-prone gardener and Blondin the brandy-swilling squirrel. This witty and stylish tale will have animal-lovers giggling to the very last page.

THE
NEW BOY

From the bestselling author of *Cats In The Belfry*

DOREEN TOVEY

THE NEW BOY

Doreen Tovey

£6.99
Paperback

ISBN 10: 1 84024 517 4
ISBN 13: 978 1 84024 517 2

The Toveys are no strangers to disaster, particularly the Siamese-related kind, but when their beloved Solomon dies unexpectedly, they're faced with a completely new type of problem – do they find another cat to replace the one they've lost?

The animals always win in the Tovey household. It is with the interests of Solomon's (very audibly) grieving sister Sheba at heart that Doreen and Charles set off in search of Solomon Secundus, affectionately known as Seeley.

Joined by a myriad of endearing characters, Seeley ensures he's living up to Solomon's standards in just the amount of time it takes to fall in a fishpond. This is an enchanting tale that will tickle your funny bone and tug on your heartstrings.

www.summersdale.com